THE
WORLD OF MUSIC

Man's
Earliest Music

THE
WORLD OF MUSIC

Man's
Earliest Music

RICHARD CARLIN

Facts On File Publications
New York, New York ● Oxford, England

Library of Congress Cataloging-in-Publication Data

Carlin, Richard.
  Man's earliest music.

  (The World of music ; v. 1)
  Bibliography: p.
  Includes index.
  Summary: Introduces music, its terms, characteristics,
role in society, and instruments, and discusses the
earliest music created by primitive people, Pacific
islanders, Africans, and American Indians.
  1. Music—History and criticism—Juvenile literature.
[1. Music—History and criticism] I. Title.
II. Series: World of music (New York, N.Y.) ; v. 1.
ML3928.C37   1986   809   85-29285
ISBN 0-8160-1324-1

Printed in the United States of America

10 9 8 7 6 5 4 3 2 1

Contents

Bowed fiddle.
PHOTO COURTESY: Roderic Knight

Preface

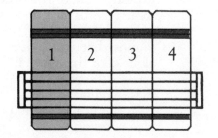

The World of Music is a series of books designed to introduce you to the different types of music found throughout the world. Each volume stands on its own as a basic introduction to a specific type of music; taken all together, the series will give a rich overview of man's musical achievements and, we hope, will inspire your own music making and listening.

Think a minute about the music in your life. On the radio, you may hear different types of music. Top 40 rock music, jazz, disco, rap, even a little classical music may all be part of your radio diet. While visiting the doctor's office or supermarket, you may hear another type of music, commonly called "Muzak." This music is meant to soothe your nerves and make you more comfortable. In school, you probably will hear another type of music: school songs, marches played by the school band at games and meets, classical music played by the school orchestra.

If during a single day you hear a classical piece by Bach and a song by the Beatles, your listening is spanning some 200 years of music making. At no other time in human history has it been possible to enjoy so many different types of music from so many different places and different times. Given all of these opportunities, it is a shame that most Americans hear only a small amount of the total world of music.

In the foothills of the Southern Appalachian mountains, traditional ballads (or long songs that tell a story) are sung today that may be a thousand years old. In the Ituri forest of central Africa, Pygmies make music that may be 50,000 years old, perhaps the oldest music heard on earth. Wherever people live, between the North and South Poles, music is being made. Fifty years ago, only explorers and adventurers were able to enjoy the music of the world's isolated peoples. No single human being could travel to visit every culture. Today, a trip to a library with a good record collection can take you around the world in minutes.

This series of books is designed to give you a general picture of each type of music. To find out more, you're going to have to explore some of the other books recommended here, and listen to some records. It's impossible for one book to say everything about a particular style of music. And words simply can't convey the sounds that you'd hear if you visited towns and cities across the globe. For this reason, I urge you to visit your library and look for some of the books and records that I'll be recommending throughout these volumes.

In the future, we're planning to expand this series to include all types of world music. For now, the following additional volumes are being produced:

English and American Folk Music: An introduction to the folk music of Great Britain and the United States, including ballads and songs, dance music, blues, church music, sea chanteys, Western swing, bluegrass, and many other topics.

European Classical Music, 1600-1850: All of the major classical composers, the development of opera, music for strings, orchestral music, church music, music notation, and many other areas.

Rock 'n' roll: The birth of rock in country and city blues, black performers of the late 40's and 50's, rockabilly (country rock 'n' roll), and many other performers and musical trends, such as Elvis Presley, Buddy Holley, Little Richard, Chuck Berry, the girl groups of the early 60's, the Beatles and the British invasion, psychedelic rock, heavy metal, soul, Michael Jackson, disco, and rap.

This first volume, which focuses on some of the earliest and most beautiful music played on earth, is a perfect starting point for your learning about the music of the world and the people who create it.

RICHARD CARLIN

1

Introduction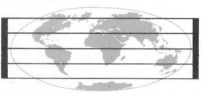

Man's Earliest Music will take you on a guided tour of four different cultures—the Pygmies of central Africa, the peoples of the Pacific islands, the Australian Aborigines, and the American Indians—taking a special look at the origins (or beginnings) of music. It examines questions about why humans make music, how music shapes our lives, and how, even within so-called "primitive" cultures, you can hear music that ranges from the simplest chant to the most complex instrumental and vocal groups.

This volume has two goals. First, it will introduce you to music, how we talk about it, where music comes from, what role it plays in a society, and the various types of musical instruments that have been developed throughout the world. Second, it will focus on four cultures that maintain some of the earliest forms of music known to humankind.

Human history can be divided into two parts: the part we know about, and the rest. Although Homo sapiens (or human beings) appeared on this planet some 500,000 years ago, written history begins only about 7,000 years ago, as far as we know. Music notation dates back only about 4,000 years, and we really only understand more modern music systems of the last 1,000 to 2,000 years. The music that we're most familiar with—Western music of the last 500 years or so—represents less than one-tenth of 1 percent of the entire history of humankind.

Since written history only began about 5000 B.C., we can't be sure how long the African Pygmies, the peoples of the Pacific islands, the Australian Aborigines, and the American Indians have inhabited this planet. The Pygmies were discovered by the Egyptians around 3000 B.C., but the other groups were simply unknown until about 1500 A.D. (only 500 years ago). This is despite the fact that many anthropologists, or people who study human history, believe these groups date back at least 50,000 years.

So, when we talk about man's earliest music, we're probably only looking at about 10,000 years of human history: from the end of the last Ice Age to today. And remember, this is not music that is only found in some museum, it is music that is performed today by peoples living all across the world. It's not one type of music, it's hundreds of different musics played by hundreds of different groups.

The music in this volume is both ancient and new. The people who make it are people both of the past and present; they live a life that was lived by humans on earth centuries ago, continuing traditions today that are believed to date back to the earliest human societies. To call this man's earliest music is not really correct, because it is also man's most recent music. It is music that remains important today for many cultures in the Pacific islands, Southeast Asia, Africa, and on American Indian reservations.

The Peoples of the World

When we think of the different peoples of the world, we might think of peoples from different countries, or peoples having different religious beliefs, or peoples with different physical characteristics, such as short versus tall peoples, or black versus white.

Anthropologists have divided the human family into four main groups: Caucasoid, Mongoloid, Negroid, and Australoid. The

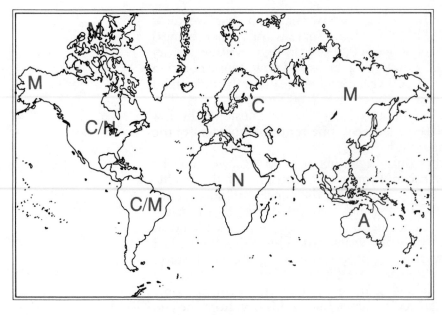

Distribution of the
World's People
C = Caucasoid
M = Mongoloid
A = Australoid
N = Negroid

Caucasoid family comprises the white-skinned European groups, including natives of the Balkans to Great Britain. Mongoloid people are described as yellow-skinned, and include Asians, Eskimos, and American Indians. The Negroids are the black-skinned peoples of Africa, now living also in the United States, the Caribbean islands, and in scattered areas throughout the world. The Australoids are the brown-skinned people of the Pacific islands and Australia.

However, not all groups fall within these handy categories. In fact, these four groups are probably no older than the last 5 to 10 thousand years. The Pygmies of Africa have been called Pygmoid peoples, because they are not members of any of these groups. And there are probably others who fall in the cracks between these four major divisions.

Many Western people divide the world into two categories: us versus them. It's easy to understand other people when they speak the same language as we do; when they enjoy the same movies, art, and music; when they live in similar homes, have similar families, and work at similar jobs. It's also easy to misunderstand people who live differently. This book will challenge you to think differently about other cultures.

What's in a Name?

When I say the word "primitive," what's the first thing that comes to your mind?

Headhunters, wearing strings of shrunken heads on their belts?

Cannibals, boiling their neighbors in a large pot, to eat for dinner?

People living in grass huts, talking to chimpanzees, and eating bananas, nuts, or anything else that they can scrape off the floor of the jungle?

Tarzan, swinging from tree to tree?

Angry Indians, attacking friendly settlers, cutting off their scalps, burning their homes, attacking helpless women and children?

There is some truth to all of these *stereotypes*, or popular ideas about primitive people. But most of these stereotypes are based on a misguided, incomplete understanding of these different cultures. In this book, we'll try to look deeper into how these so-called primitive people live, and try to understand their cultures, beliefs, and the reasons behind why they have chosen to continue to follow the traditions of their ancestors, rather than adopt more "modern" beliefs.

Remember that the word "primitive" has its roots in the Latin word *primus*, which simply means "first." Since the four groups that will be studied in this book are among the first known peoples of the Earth, it's appropriate to call them primitive. But remember also that other words have become associated with primitive people, such as backward, barbarian, crude, simple, bloodthirsty, and uncivilized.

A *stereotype* is a common image of a group of people. This image is often based on a mistaken, narrow-minded viewpoint. After a number of years, stereotypes are passed down from generation to generation, until no one knows how they originated.

It's very important to read about and listen to the music of other cultures without letting stereotypes interfere. The greatest stereotype is that, compared to European (classical) music, the music of other cultures is simple, crude, or not music at all, but simply noise. This stereotype is based on a basic misunderstanding of native musics. The Europeans who first reported that native musics of the world were simple did not themselves understand the rules of rhythm, melody, and harmony at work in these different forms of music. We can't blame them; they didn't have the ability to understand music that didn't conform to European musical rules. But the stereotype remains powerful to this day.

Other stereotypes apply to specific groups. When we think of African music, we often think of natives pounding on drums. Actually, different areas of Africa have many different types of instruments, including whistles and flutes, zithers, thumb pianos (or *mbiras*), bowed lutes, and harps, besides the drums. And, the image of natives playing drums that we often see in Tarzan movies hardly reflects either the richness of African rhythms or the wide variety of drums found in Africa.

It's easy for us to laugh at music that we don't understand, just as we sometimes laugh at behavior that seems foreign to us. Remember, though, that our musical rules, just like our rules for behavior, are simply *one* set of rules. European classical music sounds pretty silly to non-Europeans; American rock 'n' roll doesn't make any sense at all to native tribes of Australia; jazz doesn't appeal to many African natives. It takes time to learn the special rules of different forms of music, but it is worth taking this time to appreciate other approaches to harmony, rhythm, and melody. For this reason it's important to spend time learning about and listening to *different* kinds of music before forming opinions about a music that is foreign to you, whether it be European classical music or the music of Africa's Pygmies.

Music or Noise?

What's the difference between the sound of a jackhammer and the sound of an orchestra playing a Beethoven symphony? What makes some sounds music, while other sounds are noise?

First of all, music is a language, just like spoken words form a language. We can recognize a group of sounds as music because these sounds are organized or arranged in a way that only music is arranged.

Let's take an example from the English language. What's the difference between saying "I want" and "Want I"? In the first case, the words are arranged in a way that makes sense. The noun comes first, and then the verb. This is a very common organization in English. When a baby says, "I want," and points at a piece of fruit, we know that the baby wants the fruit. But, if the baby says, "Want I," we may not know what to do.

Sentences are made up by arranging groups of words in a way that makes sense or follows the rules of our language. For example, "I want a piece of fruit" makes sense, but, if we arrange the same words differently, we create non-sense: "Fruit I piece a want of."

Language takes a basic building block—the word—and puts groups of them together to form sentences. Music takes a basic building block—a sound or note—and arranges groups of them to form melodies.

There are some other clues that tell us that something is music. We often only hear music in special situations, whether it is at a concert hall or when a parent sings a child to sleep at night. Special people—called musicians or composers—make this special thing called music, and we learn to recognize their work. If a musician brings a jackhammer onto a concert hall stage and "plays" it, we might call this music, but if a construction worker is using a jackhammer on the street to break up some cement, we would never call that music.

Although many people have said that music is a universal (that is, understandable by *all* peoples) language, this isn't really true. An African Pygmy will know and like the complex rhythms of Pygmy music, but will fail to understand either Western classical music or rock 'n' roll. Similarly, we may have difficulty enjoying Pygmy music. Music really is not a single language, but a group of languages. Just as we have to learn to speak French before visiting Paris if we want to understand and to be understood, we will have to learn to listen to the various musical languages highlighted in this book.

What's Inside?

In the first part of this book, we'll be looking at some of the basic ideas about music: how music is written down (or notated), what role music plays in society, and what were the earliest musical instruments.

Chapter 2 will introduce you to some of the basic *terminology*, or words that we use to discuss music. We'll look at our modern musical notation system, or how we use dots and bars, written on five lines (called a music *staff*), to write down music. We'll discuss the problems or limitations of this system of writing music when it comes to describing the musics of other cultures. We'll define three very important terms: melody, rhythm, and harmony.

Chapter 3 takes a look at how a society is structured, from a single person, through a family, to a clan (or large family group), to a tribe. We'll look at some societies where everyone has to learn to sing songs or play musical instruments, and others where only special people are permitted to learn the musical arts. Plus we'll examine the many roles music plays in a society, from helping put

Transverse horn and gourd Ashante shrine musicians, Africa
PHOTO COURTESY: National Museum of African Art, Smithsonian Institution

babies to sleep to preparing hunters for a successful hunt, to casting a magical spell, to introducing a young man to his role as a member of the society.

Chapter 4 highlights the world of musical instruments. We'll discuss the four different groups of instruments. We'll see how the human body influenced the design of musical instruments. We'll look at the raw materials that early humans shaped into simple and then more complicated musical instruments.

The second half of the book focuses on four groups who have preserved ancient traditions: the Australian Aborigines, the Pygmies of Africa, the peoples of the Pacific islands, and the American Indians. Chapter 5 will discuss how these groups have managed to survive in the modern world. It will trace their history from the age of the European explorers, approximately 500 years ago, to the problems they face today living in a modern world. We'll look at the differences among these people, from the nomadic (or traveling) Aborigines, who have no permanent homes, to the American Indians, who developed complex civilizations, complete with villages that are linked through their own governments into tribes that form nations.

The final chapters will give you an in-depth look at each of these unique cultures. We'll try to understand their religious beliefs, rules for behavior, family life, and, most important, songs, dances, and instrumental music. We'll look at the unique musical instruments that they play. We'll discuss the unusual ways that they sing and dance, how these styles developed, and why they developed. We'll see how music plays a major role in maintaining the ancient beliefs of these peoples, even though many of them have moved away from the homes of their ancestors and now live in modern cities.

At the end of every chapter in this book, you'll find special lists of books and records. I hope this book inspires you to visit your local public library to read more about these unique cultures. More important than reading is actually listening to the music itself. Many of the records that I will mention in this book are hard to find; the big commercial record companies know that they can't make a profit issuing records of Pygmies or American Indians. For this reason, a small, dedicated group of individuals and government organizations have started companies to record this music. You'll probably be able to find these records in your public or school library.

At the end of the book, you'll find a *glossary*, or list of important words used throughout the text, with short definitions. There's also an index for quick reference to key subjects.

R·E·A·D

Brain, Robert, *The Last Primitive Peoples*. New York: Crown, 1976.

Breeden, Robert (ed.), *Primitive Worlds: People Lost in Time*. Washington, D.C.: National Geographic Society, 1973.

Sachs, Curt, *The Wellsprings of Music*. The Hague, Netherlands: Nijhoff, 1962.

Titon, Robert, *Worlds of Music*. New York: Schirmer Books, 1984.

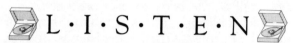

L·I·S·T·E·N

Music of the World's Peoples. Folkways 4504–4507.

Primitive Musics of the World. Folkways 4581.

2

Introduction to musical terms

Music is a special language. In order to understand it, we have to use special words to describe how music is made. In this chapter we'll discuss the basics of *music theory*, or how we talk about music. In the first part of the chapter we'll talk about scales, how we measure *intervals*, or the distance between notes, and how music is written down, or *notated*. Then we'll compare Western ideas about *melody*, *rhythm*, and *harmony* to non-Western ideas. In this way, we'll show there's more than one way to put notes together to form a musical composition.

Scales, Cents, and Intervals

Imagine a piano keyboard. Let's just look at a small section, between middle C and the next C above it.

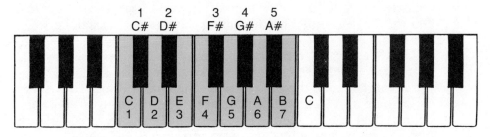

Count the number of white notes from the first C to the second C. You should see 7 white notes.

The 7 white notes make up a *scale*, in this case the C-major scale. The eighth note, or *octave* (from the Latin for "eight"), is the same as the first note, although it is higher in pitch. Try playing these notes on a piano, if you have one at home.

Now count the number of black notes. There are 5. Seven white notes plus 5 black notes equals 12. This is called a 12-tone scale.

Let's give each note a value of 100 points. C equals 0, C-sharp (the first black note next to it) equals 100, D (the next note after that) equals 200, and so on.

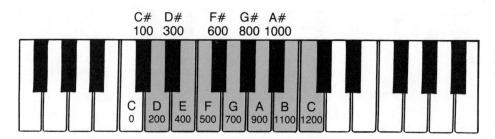

We can call these points "cents," because *centum* is the Latin word for one hundred.

Look between the notes C and C-sharp. There's a crack in the piano keyboard. In this crack, you can imagine 99 cents appearing. There are 99 other tones between C and C-sharp that you can never hear on a piano. (Actually, we could further divide these 99 cents into smaller and smaller parts. If we continued to do this, we would create an infinite number of smaller tones between C and C-sharp.)

This system of cents was developed by British physicist Alexander Ellis (1814-1890) in an attempt to describe non-Western scales. Ellis had a set of tuning forks made, each tuned to a specific note, so he could accurately analyze the tones produced by instruments collected from all over the world. The result was a very practical and easy-to-use system for describing those notes that fall between the cracks of the Western 12-tone scale.[*]

This Western 12-tone scale, with each tone separated by 100 cents, developed over hundreds of years. It's called an *equally tempered* scale, because the gaps between the notes (from C to C-sharp or G-sharp to A) are all equal; each one is exactly 100 cents. Before equal temperament, there were scales that featured unequal intervals or gaps between the notes. To understand how this scale developed, let's look briefly at two basic intervals, the octave and the fifth.

---

[*]Cents measure the interval or space between tones; they don't tell us the pitch of the tone. This pitch, or frequency, is described in a number that represents vibrations per second (vps). For instance, in European concert pitch, A above middle-C is tuned to 440 vps.

Intervals

An *interval* is the space between any two scale notes. The space between C and the next C above it is called an *octave*. Imagine you have a 12-inch string in your hand. When you pluck it, the note C sounds. Now, let's divide the string exactly in half. A string 6-inches long produces another C, but it is an octave higher than the first C. Now, let's make the string twice as long. This string produces a C also, but it is an octave lower than the first C.

The *ratio* or relation between the first C and the C an octave above it is 2 to 1 (the string is twice as long when the first C sounds [2], than when the second C sounds [1]).

If we divide the string into thirds, we can hear another basic interval. Imagine we divide our 12-inch string into one section that is 4-inches long, and another section that is 8-inches long. Remember that the 12-inch string played a C. The 8-inch section will now play a G.

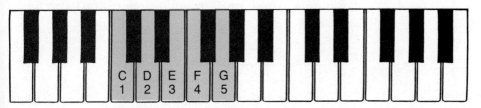

Count the white keys on the piano from C to G. You'll see that G is five notes above C; so this interval is called a fifth.

Thousands of years ago, the Chinese took these two simple intervals and used them as the basis for creating their scales. They started with one tone, which they called the "Yellow Bell." Then, they found the note a fifth above it. They then continued higher and higher, either by fifths or octaves. You may not realize it, but if you continue up the scale, starting at C, traveling by fifths, you will find all the other scale notes:

C—G—D—A—E—B—F#—C#—G#—D#—A#—F—C

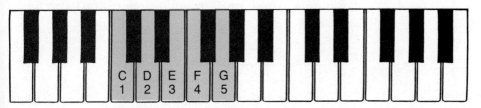

This is called the *circle of fifths*.

Why all this talk about cents, octaves, and fifths? Because all cultures have based their music on these very simple relationships. And once we realize that the notes that we have chosen to make up our scales are based on making a selection out of 1,200 possible tones (if not more), we can better understand the decisions made by other cultures.

Notation

Music notation developed in the West from about 1200 A.D. to today. There are other systems of notation that have developed in the world, notably in China, India, and Japan, not to mention systems of tablature notation for individual instruments developed in both the West and other cultures.

It's important for us to be familiar with Western notation and how it works. To begin with, a music *staff* consists of five parallel lines. We can number these lines, from bottom to top, 1 to 5:

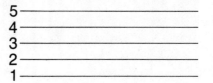

At the left-hand side of this staff appears a *clef*. The clef tells us the range of notes that can be written on the staff. The most common clefs are G clef (or treble clef) and F clef (or bass clef). Treble clef is called G clef because the tail of the clef wraps around the second line of the staff, where the note G is written:

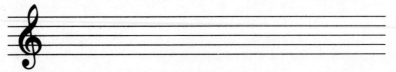

Bass clef is called F clef because the two dots next to the clef embrace the fourth line of the staff, where the F is written:

These two clefs are most often seen in piano music, the top line giving the treble (usually melody) part, while the bottom line gives the bass (usually accompaniment) part:

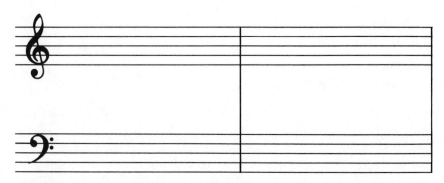

Let's bring back the piano keyboard. Starting at middle C, we can show the notes on the treble clef as they correspond to the keyboard:

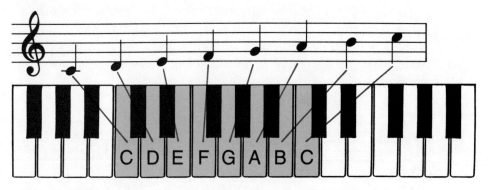

Notes below middle C are generally written on the bass clef. Here's those notes, from middle C down one octave:

You'll notice that middle C falls outside of the staff proper. Notes can be written above the staff, to extend its range up, or below the clef to extend its range down.

Notes indicate more than just pitch. They also indicate duration, or time value. Here are the basic notes and their time values, with their common names:

Whole note   o

Half note   ♩

Quarter note   ♩
Eighth note   ♪
Sixteenth note   ♬
Thirty-second note   ♬

Notice that as we work down this list, we are dividing each note into smaller and smaller parts. For example, 2 half notes equal one whole note, 2 quarter notes equal one half note (therefore, 4 quarter notes equal one whole note), 2 eighth notes equal one quarter note (how many eighth notes equal a half note? whole note?), and so on.

Time Signature and Key Signature

At the left side of the staff, next to the clef, you'll often see two other important symbols. One is the *time signature* and the other is the *key signature*. The time signature gives the definition of the basic rhythm of a piece of music. Here are some common time signatures:

Measures were developed in Western musical notation in order to make it easier to read music. The time signature tells us how many beats are in each measure, and how long to hold each different (type of note. For example, in ¼ time, the top number tells us that there are four beats to a measure, while the bottom number tells us that a quarter note receives one beat. In this time signature, an eighth note receives half a beat, because an eighth note always has half the value of a quarter note.

In ¾ time, there are 3 beats to a measure, and each quarter note receives 1 beat.

However, in ⅝ time, there are 6 beats to a measure, but an eighth note receives one beat. A quarter note receives 2 beats (Why?).

The *key signature* identifies the key or scale that is being used in a piece of music. It indicates which notes have to be raised (*sharp*) or lowered (*flat*) in tone in order to make a 7-note major or minor scale.

Let's loot again at the C scale. The distance between C and D is called a *whole step* (WS), because there's another note (C#)

between C and D. The distance between D and E is another whole step, but between E and F is only a *half step* (HS), because there is no other note between them. If we continue up the scale, we find this pattern:

WS—WS—HS—WS—WS—WS—HS
C-D D-E E-F F-G G-A A-B B-C

Let's look at a different scale or key. Start on the piano keyboard at G, using this same pattern. G to A is a whole step; A to B is another WS; B to C is a half step (just like E and F in the C scale); C to D is a WS; D to E is a WS; but E to F is only a HS (and we need a WS here), so we substitute F# for F; and F# to G is a HS.

All 7-note major scales follow this pattern. In order to get our WS-WS-HS-WS-WS-WS-HS pattern, we have to raise or lower certain notes, depending on where we start on the piano keyboard. Minor scales (and other types of scales) all have their own special patterns.

Problems with Western Notation

It's important to remember that our system of notation was developed for our music. There are many problems when it comes to notating the music of other cultures. For instance, let's take an example where C equals O cents and C# equals 100 cents. We hear an Australian Aborigine sing 2 notes and record them on our tape machine. When we take this recording to a laboratory, an analysis shows that the interval, or gap, between the two notes is equal to 48 cents. To make matters worse, the singer sings with *vibrato*, or a quavering sound in his voice. The interval actually varies between 40 cents at the lowest sound of the second tone and 55 cents at its highest sound, but most frequently rests around 48 cents. How can we notate these two pitches?

The answer is we simply can't. Western notation doesn't make allowances for notes that fall between the cracks of the 12-tone scale. Nor does it make allowances for vibrato, even though Western singing features vibrato (There are very specialized marks for vibrato, but these indicate the specialized vibrato found in Western music—in opera, for example—and our Australian may not use this type of vibrato). To notate non-Western music, we would ideally have to develop special notation systems for each type of music.

Melody, Rhythm, and Harmony

Music is often described in terms of three basic elements:

1. Melody
2. Rhythm
3. Harmony

Let's consider the first two elements, from a Western musical perspective.

Western Ideas

The *melody* is a collection of notes organized in a specific pattern to form a total musical thought.

Rhythm or *meter* tells us how much time each note will be held or played.

A simple melody can be built on repetitions of very short phrases; for example, here's a melody that you probably know "Three Blind Mice":

Look at the first four measures. The first and second measure are identical; the third and fourth measure are identical. How about the next four measures? The fifth, sixth, and seventh measures are identical. The eighth measure is the same as the first. And then the entire melody is repeated.

Now let's look at the *intervals*. This melody is based on the C scale. Let's isolate the most important notes.

The interval between E and C is called a *third* (because E is the third note in the C scale). This is the first important interval.

The interval between G and C is a *fifth*. This is the next important interval. The interval or space between G and E is also a third (because there's a note, F, between them; count the keys E-F-G and you get there).

The interval between C and the next C is called an *octave*. This is the last important interval.

Isolating these intervals, we have the 1st-3rd-5th-8th tones of the scale. The 1-3-5 notes make up a C *chord*. A chord is the basis of the last important element of music, *harmony*.

In Western music, harmony is written to be played along with a melody. It can be based either on single notes or groups of notes played at the same time.

Try holding down middle C and the next white key, D, at the same time. The sound you hear probably doesn't sound very pleasant to you. This interval is called a second (Do you know why?). Now hold down C and the next white key, E. This is a third. This probably sounds a little better. Now hold down C, E, and G (We're skipping F). You're hearing a C-major chord. This probably sounds very good to you.

There are many other types of chords and harmonies in Western music that we could discuss. However, we want to compare our Western notions of melody, rhythm, and harmony with non-Western ideas.

Non-Western Ideas

When we Westerners think of melody, rhythm, and harmony, we usually think of one melody line, accompanied by one harmony part, all in the same rhythm. This need not be the case.

Music is written both vertically (in a straight line) or horizontally (with parts added on top of each other). A melody in Western music is usually vertical; it starts at the first measures, moves ahead through a series of measures until it reaches the last measure, and either stops or repeats. A melody that moves vertically and then repeats can also be pictured as circular, because it has a beginning, middle, and end, and then returns to the same beginning to repeat the pattern.

You're probably familiar with the *round*. In this form of music, one person starts singing a melody. A second person starts the same melody after waiting for the first singer to complete either 1, 2, or 4 measures. A third singer may come in after the second singer has completed 1, 2, or 4 measures, and other singers could join in in the same manner following the third singer. Each individual part is circular, and can be sung as long as the individual singers want to keep on going. The entire round can be described as being written horizontally; the parts are stacked up on top of each other.

and so on

Melody

Melody, which is so important to us, is not always the most important element in non-Western music. In some American Indian chants, for example, the melody consists of a single note repeated over and over. Chants are often used to bring about an almost dreamlike state in the listener and the singer. Why would a one-note melody achieve this goal better than a more elaborate melody?

Of course, it's somewhat misleading to call these Indian chants "one-note melodies." The singer will often embellish the note with vibrato, dipping slightly above or below the basic pitch; the note may be interrupted with other sounds, such as a deep exhalation (letting out breath) or some other nonvocal sound such as clicking the tongue. None of these sounds fall into our Western ideas of "notes," but they are all part of this melody.

Non-Western melodies are often based on ther repetition of short, simple phrases (or groups of notes), just like "Three Blind Mice." While Western listeners sometimes find repetition boring, many non-Western cultures find that repetition helps build intensity into their music.

Scales

Non-Western singers don't use Western scales. In our earlier example, "Three Blind Mice" is based on the C scale. Let's look at an example from an Australian Aboriginal tribe:

Australian Aborigine Song from *Tribal Music of Australia* (Folkways 4439).

How can we tell what scale this music is in? We can begin by counting the number of different notes in the piece. The note that occurs most often is called the pitch center. By counting all of the notes, we can also find the melodic range (how far the melody moves beyond the pitch center either up or down the scale). In this example, it so happens that there are 15 Cs. The next most common note is the F, followed by the G, D, E, and finally the A.

Because this scale has 6 notes, it is called a *hexatonic* scale (from the Greek words "hexa" [6] and "tonic" [tone]). A common non-Western scale is the *pentatonic* scale (5-note scale; from the Greek "penta" [5]).

In this example, the intervals are all seconds (C-D-E-F-G-A), just as in the Western C-major scale. However, this need not be the case. Many non-Western scales have gaps; for instance, the scale might be C-D#-F#-A-B. This is also a pentatonic scale, because it has 5 notes, even though these notes are not next to each other on the piano keyboard.

Keeping the Beat

Non-Western rhythms tend to be more complicated than Western music. The song "Three Blind Mice" is *isometric*; each measure is the same length, and has the same basic beat. There are many examples of isometric rhythms in non-Western music, too. However, there are also examples of *heterometric* rhythms, where the length of the measures will change within a single piece.

Crow singer/drummer
PHOTO COURTESY: Smithsonian Institution, Natl. Anthropological Archives

Non-Western music often features *polyrhythm*, or more than one rhythm being played at the same time. For example, there is a recording of a Melanesian group performing a dance. The song that the dancers are singing is in one rhythm. Their stamping feet forms an entirely different rhythmic pattern. Meanwhile, four different accompanists beat out four other rhythms on sticks. The result is a piece with six different rhythms being played at once.

Many African tribes build complicated polyrhythms by taking simple drum patterns and laying them on top of each other. Each drummer plays a pattern that repeats over and over. He works independently of the other drummers, each of whom has his own pattern. The result is a dense pattern of rhythms.

The meter or rhythm of a specific piece of music can be described as *divisive* or *additive*. In most Western music, we use divisive rhythms: $\frac{2}{4}$, $\frac{4}{4}$, $\frac{6}{8}$, $\frac{3}{4}$. In each of these examples, the number of beats per measure is either 2 ($\frac{2}{4}$, $\frac{4}{4}$, $\frac{6}{8}$) or 3 ($\frac{3}{4}$, $\frac{9}{8}$). In additive rhythms, each measure can vary in length; one measure might be $\frac{5}{4}$, the next $\frac{7}{4}$, the next $\frac{13}{4}$, and on and on. A single song could include both types of rhythm.

Divisive rhythms are usually based on either 2 beats per measure (called duple rhythms) or 3 beats per measure (called triple rhythms). Musicologists make a further distinction between simple duple or triple rhythms and compound duple or triple rhythms.

Both simple and compound duple rhythms have 2 beats per measure. In simple duple rhythm, the beat can be further divided by twos into smaller parts. For example, in $\frac{2}{4}$ time, a quarter note is held for 1 beat. The quarter note can be further divided by 2 into 2 eighth notes, 4 sixteenth notes, 8 thirty-second notes, and so on.

$$\frac{2}{4}$$

In compound duple time, the beat is further divided by threes into smaller parts. For instance, in $\frac{6}{8}$ time, a dotted quarter corresponds to 1 beat. This can be further divided into 3 eighth notes, 6 sixteenth notes, 12 thirty-second notes, and so on.

$$\frac{6}{8}$$

The same holds true for simple and compound triple times, except now there are 3 beats per measure. In $\frac{3}{4}$ time, a quarter equals 1 beat, and the beat can be subdivided into 2 eighths, 4 sixteenths, and so on.

$$\frac{3}{4}$$

Can you work out the values in the compound triple time signature of $\frac{9}{8}$?

Harmony

Non-Western music again has its own approach to harmony. In *monophonic* vocal music, a group of singers all sing the same melody line (*mono* means "one," *phonic* means "melody"). *Polyphonic* music (*poly* means "many") features more than one part. "Harmony" is one type of polyphony; this is when a second singer or group of singers sings another part that has the same rhythm but does not have the same notes; this is called *homophonic* music. Many non-Westerners like the sound of what we would consider to be unusual harmonies; for example, natives of the Balkans sing songs in parallel seconds (in other words, one singer sings "C" while the other sings "D").

Heterophony is the term that Western musicians have given to pieces where the two parts seem to be unrelated. In other words, one person sings one melody in one rhythm. Usually, the melodies are similar, but there is some variation in either pitch or rhythm between the two singers (or groups of singers). Again, we can imagine several different parts going at once, with maybe 10 different singers all singing slightly different melodies or rhythms.

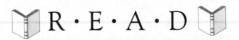

R · E · A · D

Craig, Jean, *The Story of Musical Notes*. Minneapolis: Lerner, 1962.
Evans, Roger, *How to Read Music*. New York: Crown, 1978.

Music in society

We're seated in a concert hall. On stage, a symphony orchestra is assembled; various members are tuning their instruments, chatting with their neighbors, or adjusting the music on their stands. Everyone in the audience is well dressed; the men wear jackets and ties, while the women wear gowns. When the conductor steps out onto the stage, the lights dim and the crowd quiets. When he reaches the podium, the audience responds with polite applause. The conductor turns his back on the audience, and lifts his arms to signal the orchestra that they should prepare to begin their performance.

*   *   *   *

We're visiting a Pygmy camp in the Ituri forest in central Africa. During the evening, the men begin their special festival of singing and dancing, called the *molimo*. The old men gather in a secret place and sing, while the young men dance. No one is allowed to sleep, and no one is allowed to stop singing; otherwise the festival will lack its intended effect, to bring happiness and health to the Pygmy tribe. Women are prohibited from attending the festival or even hearing the songs. While the men sing, we are suddenly aware of voices answering in the forest, and the distant sound of a horn. The horn imitates both the songs that the men are singing and also strange animal noises. As the dawn nears, the sound of the horn player comes closer and closer and closer, until finally a large group of young Pygmies enter the camp, playing loudly on the horn and moving wildly between the other tribesmen.

*   *   *   *

We are in a giant football stadium. Laser beams are flashing across the sky. Suddenly, two smoke bombs erupt and a caped singer leaps onto the stage. The audience erupts into spontaneous clapping, yelling, and dancing as music fills the air. A group of young girls tries to storm the stage, but they are held back by armed bodyguards. The performer dances around the stage, while his image is projected on giant screens above him. The music is so loud that it seems to push against us, as if it had a physical force. At the end of the concert, thousands of balloons are released from overhead, and the fans cheer wildly.

* * * *

I have just described three very different types of musical performances. The first and third examples are obviously concerts as they occur today in the United States or Europe; the second description is of an important ceremony in the life of an African community. Obviously, these three very different types of concerts have to be judged in different ways.

In our modern society, music is performed only on special occasions, such as at a concert. In other cultures, music is performed throughout the workday, as part of everyday tasks such as hunting, gathering food, nursing children, playing games, or even just relaxing. While in our culture special people, called musicians, perform music, in other cultures everyone has some musical talent and is expected to contribute to the music making.

At first glance, it may appear that music has a very small role in our lives. Still, there remain some clues as to the importance of music in our society. There are many musical compositions that we hear almost every day. "Happy Birthday" is sung to celebrate an individual's birthdate; "Taps" is played on the bugle to mark the death of an important individual; "Hail to the Chief" is played when the President appears in public; hymns are sung at church services, while special songs are saved for specific holy days; Christmas carollers go from door-to-door at Christmastime, while "Auld Lang Syne" has become associated with New Year's Eve; "Pomp and Circumstance," a 19th-century march written by Edward Elgar, is now played at almost every high school and college graduation. This list could go on and on.

The music is so much a part of our lives that we may not even notice its presence, or give a second thought to its meaning. Why is music such an important part of these individual and national ceremonies? Why must every nation have its own national anthem? Why do popular performers choose a "theme song," such as "Thanks for the Memories" for Bob Hope?

Many of the answers can be found as we examine tribal musics of the world. In the tribe, music is such a central part of life that many tribes don't even have a word for music. They never talk about music separated from the everyday life of the tribe. Music serves a function for entertainment; as work songs; to mark specific rituals in an individual's life; to mark specific achievements of the tribe; to make a religious ritual work; to contact the gods of the earth; to celebrate special days in the year.

In this chapter, we will explore the many ways that music plays a role in the social life of a group of people. We will draw on examples from all around the globe, including contemporary America. In this way, we hope to show that music is more than just something that entertains or soothes us; it is an important part of our individual and group well-being.

Society and Culture

Before there were societies, there were individual men and women, roaming the earth. When a man and woman mated, they formed the basis of a family. The relation between the man and woman and their children was a special one, even if they went on to have other relationships with other people.

The basic social unit is the family (man-woman-children). As the children have their own children, the family is extended (grandparents-parents-children). As the brothers and sisters of each child have their own families, the family is further extended (grandparent-parent-aunt/uncle-children). In this way, a family grows into an "extended family," or clan, a group of closely and/or not-so-closely related people.

Not all groups of people maintain families in the way that I've just described them. Some groups may view a man and his wives as a family, or a woman and her husbands, or a group of men and women who have mated in the past (or continue to mate in the present) as a family. Although the family is based on a biological (or natural) need to create children, it is not only a biological unit. In some cultures, a child's uncle is given the same respect as the father. In fact, there is no distinction between the two, even though members of these cultures realize that the uncle is not the biological, or natural, father. The family is a social unit; we come to look at our fathers, mothers, children, and spouses as friends, companions, or hunting partners, as well as our blood relatives.

As family or clans grow, they may become associated, particularly if they live in the same geographic area. The relationship among clans may be one of rivalry, where each clan seeks to maintain its own individual power whether it be in land, food, hunting rights, or material goods such as farming or hunting implements, or even homes. Another potential relationship is one of working together for mutual benefit. A larger area can be farmed if there are more farmhands; it may be physically impossible for one family to raise

Classical concert and Rock concert

enough children to manage a bigger area. A larger group working together can also hunt larger animals, which one or two people could not hope to kill or capture.

Another possible organization is that of the *tribe*. A tribe is usually defined as a group of clans or families, linked together in an organized manner. There is usually a leader, or a group of leaders, who may either be the oldest members of the clans or the most talented. The tribe usually has common beliefs or practices; that is, they share certain rituals, whether they be rules for when a young person can become a full member of the tribe, or celebrations to show thanks for a good harvest of crops and also to appease a spirit believed to have power over the harvest.

Tribes then are based on something that goes far beyond blood relationship, because not all members are necessarily related. The elements that distinguish each tribe are called, as a group, its *culture*. In 1871, Edward Burnett Taylor, in an important book called *Primitive Culture*, gave a definition for culture that remains useful today: "Culture . . . includes knowledge, belief, art, morals, law, custom, and any other capabilities and habits acquired by man as a member of society."

Culture is *not* inherited. If an Australian Aborigine were raised in New York City by a well-to-do family, he or she would not grow up hunting wild game. Nor would this Aborigine know anything about the rites and rituals of the Aborigine tribes. Similarly, an American baby deposited in an Aborigine tribe would not grow up reading the *New York Times*. Our beliefs, customs, and ways of behaving, which we take so much for granted, are learned by us throughout our lives. In fact, we are always adjusting to new beliefs and customs.

The Musician

The role of the musician in a society differs from culture to culture. First of all, when we talk about musicians, we're talking about a specialized class of people whose primary role in life is to play music. In Western society, we will often describe our friends or family members by their occupation or the job that they perform: You might say, "My mother is a doctor," or "My brother is a teacher," or "My friend is a member of a rock band."

However, in other societies, all members of the society may be expected to do a variety of jobs. For example, in a hunting and gathering group of Aborigines, every member of the tribe has to help with the search for food; otherwise, the tribe would starve. Although there are special functions that only men or women perform, all members of the tribe also share general jobs such as gathering food.

In some societies, everyone is expected to be musical, so that there is no separate group of musicians. For example, in an Aborigine tribe everyone would participate in singing hunting or gathering songs. No one would really say "But I can't sing," or "I'm not a professional musician." These songs are part of the shared culture of the tribe and, more important, they help guarantee the success of the hunt or search for food. For this reason, failure of any one person to participate in singing could lead to group disaster.

In other tribes, some music may be performed communally (or as a group), while other music is performed only by a special class of professional musicians. When we talk about professional musicians in the West, we mean people who earn their living by playing music. In our society, we judge success in terms of money or material goods. For example, a famous rock star might be paid half a million dollars to play a series of concerts, while a lesser known group just breaking in might only be paid several hundred dollars for the same concerts.

In other cultures, musicians are also paid to perform, although this payment may not be in money. In a tribe that has a chief or is governed by a group of elders, the governing group may support a musician by providing him* with food and shelter. Or a family or clan might pay for a musician's services at a funeral or important family occasion. Or the members of the tribe might simply recognize the musician as a special, talented person. In some cases, musicians are allowed to live outside of the laws governing other members of the tribe, because they are viewed as special people. For this reason, they may not be punished for robbery, murder, or other crimes, because without the musicians, the society could not function.

In our Western society, a person can become a musician in many different ways. For example, you could attend a college of music, if you wished to perform classical music. After years of training, you would audition for an orchestra and, if you were extremely

---

*In most cases, professional musicians in these cultures are male.

lucky, be accepted as a member. If you want to be a rock 'n' roll star, you would have to form a band and "pay your dues" by playing in many small clubs. If you're lucky, you would be "discovered" by an agent and signed by a major record company.

In non-Western society, there are also many routes to becoming a musician. In some cultures, a person must be born into a musical family in order to become a musician. This is true of many African societies, which have developed special roles for each person in the society. The musical spirit is believed to be passed on from father to son (in some societies, a mother from a musical family can pass on her talents to a son as well). Because music comes from the spiritual world and the power to make music is given only to a few families, it would be unacceptable for someone outside of a musical family to suddenly decide to be a musician.

In other societies, anyone can become a musician. Talent is still believed to come from a spiritual or otherworldly source; but, in these cultures, it is believed that this talent is distributed equally among all the members of the group. For this reason, these societies may produce more music, simply because there are more potential musicians.

Some world cultures have developed Western-style professional musicians as more tourists have come to visit their people. For example, in Hawaii, almost all native music is now performed for visitors, either at hotels, nightclubs, or even in airport lounges. This music has naturally been influenced by Western rock 'n' roll and pop sounds, and has very little to do with the original Hawaiian music. The musicians who play it work for money and are totally separated from their tribes; in fact, the sense of cultural or tribal identity has virtually disappeared, as individual tribe members have moved into the cities to live a more Westernized life-style.

It is tempting for Westerners to view a society as more advanced when it develops professional musicians. After all, as people take special roles they should become more talented at performing their jobs, and should do a better job. In our Western culture, we not only have doctors, we have specialists who perform only one small medical task, but do it extremely well. Similarly, you wouldn't ask a classical violinist to play fiddle in a bluegrass band or to try to play electric violin in a rock 'n' roll group.

On the other hand, you could view this Western specialization as less developed than other cultures. After all, when everyone could play music, everyone shared a very special knowledge. Nowadays, many Westerners can only play the radio—they know very little about music. Isn't a society more advanced when everyone has knowledge about how to actually perform a task, rather than just how to watch (or listen to) it?

The Use and Function of Music

Musicologists make a distinction between how music is *used* in a society and how it *functions*. Let's take a simple example.

You set your clock radio to play music to wake you up in the morning. This music has only one *use*, to wake you up. Its *function* can be described in larger terms: In order for our society to continue to grow, you need to attend school or go to a job. Without the clock radio, you wouldn't wake up on time. The school or work day would be disrupted; you would miss learning important information, or fail to perform an important job. Other peoples' lives would be disrupted, either your co-workers or classmates. The function of this music, then, is to keep an important part of society on schedule.

Let's take another example. A composer writes a jingle for Big Ed's Hamburgers. This jingle is used to sell hamburgers for Big Ed. Its function is varied; if the tune is pleasant, it can be simply entertaining. In a larger sense, by promoting the sales of Big Ed's Hamburgers, the song helps promote our social system, which is based on buying and selling products. By purchasing hamburgers, we're putting money into the hands of Big Ed, who will hire more people, build more restaurants, and generally help the community. As more people are employed, more people can afford to eat out, and so Big Ed will prosper.

Musician or Composer?

In Western society, musicians may or may not compose or write their own music. We usually expect classical performers to play the works of other composers, such as Bach or Beethoven. In rock 'n' roll, we value more highly those performers who compose their own music. In jazz, we often expect the performer to offer a personal interpretation of pieces written by other composers.

In non-Western music, there are various attitudes toward composing, and different ideas concerning what composing a piece of music means. These different ideas may exist within a single society (just as we have different attitudes toward classical, rock, and jazz musics).

Musicologists distinguish three sources for music: individual composition, spiritual sources, or other humans (either other members of the society or from outside of the society). Depending on the values of a given culture, these different sources will all be drawn on for new compositions.

An individual composition is any piece of music written by a single person or group of people working together. For instance, Bach sat down and wrote the Brandenberg Concerti. John Lennon and Paul McCartney together wrote many songs, including "Please, Please Me." Not only must individual humans write these songs, they must be credited as the authors. In other words, their friends, relatives, and other members of the tribe must recognize that the piece of music was written by them.

A piece of music with spiritual sources is said to come from either the gods, spirits, or other nonhumans. For example, many Irish dance tunes are said to be the compositions of fairies or trolls. Musicians and listeners will say, "This tune came from the little people." The performer does not take credit for writing the dance tune. In some African cultures, all music is said to come from the spiritual world. Thus, when a performer plays a new piece of music he is actually just transmitting (or carrying) the music of the spiritual world to our world. He takes no credit as composer, recognizing that all music comes from the gods.

Occasionally, an isolated tribe or group of people will come into contact with another group whom they have never seen before. Often, singers will sit together and trade their songs. Any song learned from another musician, whether or not that musician is the composer, has as its source another person.

In Western cultures, we often think of a composition as something that is entirely new. For instance, a song should have unique words and music. Sometimes a songwriter will base a song on some earlier melody or set of words. However, there has to be enough new about the song for us to consider it an original composition.

In non-Western societies, a person may claim to have composed a song when all that he has done is slightly changed the lyrics of a song that has been known for generations. This process of building on a tradition is natural in a culture that values the past. Musicians/composers are not expected to create entirely new pieces of music; it would be too hard for the other members of the society to quickly learn new songs.

The Role of Music

Music plays a vital role in many cultures. We've already touched on some of the many roles it can play in our own and other societies. It is impossible to describe every possible role, because we would have to investigate every society. Some societies have very specialized needs. Alan Merriam, a musicologist who spent his life studying African music, describes how the Watusi, whose entire society depends on cattle raising for its survival, have developed appropriate music for their special needs.

After many years of study, Merriam and others have developed some simple categories to describe the different types of music that have developed in socieities.

Work and welfare relates to music developed to aid basic tasks, such as grinding corn or paddling a canoe. Songs can help keep a work crew working at the same speed, which helps them work more effectively. If four men are paddling a boat, it's important that they all dip their oars and pull back at the same time; otherwise, they won't get very far.

Social institutions relates to all of the important functions of a society. Songs that help prepare the men for war or to build group spirit during a particularly difficult period help to hold the society together. Songs that commemorate the famous deeds of past members of the tribe help build group pride and identity.

Life cycle relates to the journey from childhood to mature adult. Cultures have developed songs related to every new experience, including lullabies to help the baby to sleep, to songs that teach the child about tribal traditions, even to toilet-training songs! Members of the Tonga tribe in western Polynesia have composed children's songs that are used in a juggling game called *hiko*. In this game, the child juggles as many as six balls, and the song helps him to keep track of the balls and to keep the proper rhythm going. The child is also learning mathematics by playing this game.

Other songs cover the rest of the life cycle. When the male child reaches puberty, he is ready to join the adult males as a member of the tribe. In some groups, this *initiation* occurs in stages; in others, it is a single, one-time ceremony. (The Jewish ceremony of *Bar Mitzvah* is an initiation ceremony.) Special music marks this

Single-stringed plucked lutes Hausa tribe, Africa
PHOTO COURTESY: Natl. Museum of African Art,
Smithsonian Institution

occasion. When the man is ready to marry, music marks this event. Finally, when death comes to a tribal member, special music is performed to commemorate his achievements and to lay his soul at rest.

Religious institutions describes music used in any religious ceremony, whether it be to contact dead ancestors, appease the spiritual world, or celebrate a specific religious holiday.

Control of power is closely related to the religious category. This includes songs used to influence the supernatural world. In many societies, human life is thought to be directly influenced by spirits. For example, the failure of a human being in battle is believed to be caused by the anger of a spiritual being. Or the failure of a year's crop may be seen as being caused by the displeasure of the gods. For this reason, songs can be used to magically influence the spiritual world to help humans. Songs can also be used to influence other human beings. For example, some tribes believe certain people have magical powers to cast spells on other members of the group, causing disease or death. Music can be used to break these spells.

Enjoyment/entertainment includes all music that is used simply to entertain. Because music is so important throughout non-Western cultures, we tend to think that all music has some purpose. But tribal people enjoy music for its own sake, just as we do.

Finally, *language* includes music that is specifically created to preserve important texts. For instance, songs that tell tribal history, or the story of the creation of the earth, or the feats of a single person all have the function of preserving important information. In nonliterate cultures, where people can't read, the best way to preserve history is to put it into song. Songs play another important role: In some tribes, a chieftain can't be directly criticized. However, a singer may be allowed to sing a satirical song that contains a critical message. Songs can also tell about current events in societies that don't have newspapers, television, or radio.

R·E·A·D

Hood, Mantle, *The Ethnomusicologist*. New York: McGraw-Hill, 1971.
Merriam, Alan P., *The Anthropology of Music*. Evanston, IL: Northwestern University Press, 1964.

Musical instruments

In this chapter we'll see how musical instruments are *classified*, or put into different groups. We'll discuss how the human body influenced the design of musical instruments; how musical instruments produce sounds; and some of the earliest musical instruments and how they work. We'll ask: How do we know which instruments are the oldest? We'll look at how humans shaped natural materials, such as bamboo, into music makers.

Types of Musical Instruments

In order to understand the differences among various musical instruments, its important to be able to separate them into groups, or to *classify* them. Musical instruments can be classed by where they are found in the world, what material they are made of (brass, wood, vegetable gourds, stone), when they were developed, or how they produce sounds. This last method is probably the simplest, since it includes instruments from different cultures. As it happens, there already exists a simple classification system based on this idea.

The Sachs/von Hornbostel System

In 1914, pioneer musicologists Erich von Hornbostel and Curt Sachs created a simple means of dividing the musical instruments of the world, both Western and non-Western, into four categories. Although some have challenged this system, it remains useful today. The categories are:

Playing clappers called *thiski*.
Baiga tribe, India
PHOTO COURTESY: Roderic Knight

1. Idiophones
2. Membranophones
3. Chordophones
4. Aerophones*

Although these seem like imposing terms at first, they really are quite simple. The suffix "phone" comes from the Greek *phon*, simply meaning "sound." Each prefix indicates what element of the musical instrument makes the sound. Let's take the groups one at a time.

In describing these categories, I will be using many modern examples, because you are probably more familiar with Western musical instruments than those played in other parts of the world. However, I will also try to introduce some of the older instruments that we will be exploring in this volume.

IDIOPHONES

The term *idio/phone* combines the Greek *idio* (meaning "self") with *phon* (meaning "sound"). In these instruments, the total body of the instrument vibrates to make a sound. A very simple example would be a gong. When a musician strikes a gong with a mallet, the entire surface of the gong vibrates to make the sound. This would be called a *struck idiophone* in the von Hornbostel/Sachs system.

Other examples of idiophones would be xylophones, bells, rasps, and shakers (maracas). Sachs and von Hornbostel noted that idiophones can be struck, plucked, rubbed (work by friction), or

---

*Sachs added a fifth category, electrophones, in the 1940's, to include modern electronic instruments.

IDIOPHONES

Struck

2 Objects struck together (*Clappers*)
- Rhythm sticks
- Castanets

1 Object struck with a stick or by hand:
- Tubes
  —slit-drum
- Solid
  —xylophone

Shaken

Rattles
- Seeds or stones placed inside of a container (gourd rattles)
- Stones or seeds strung on a thin string and held in a frame (yoke rattles)

Friction (Scraped)

Notched sticks (One stick rubbed against another stick)

Plucked

Jew's harp
Mbira or "thumb piano"

MEMBRANOPHONES

Drums

Frame (narrow hoop covered with skin)
Cylinder (hollow branch or tube)
Hourglass
Kettle

Singing

Thin membrane that alters the sound of the voice
- the kazoo

CHORDOPHONES

Zithers

Musical bow
Raft zither (single tubes, each supporting a single string, tied together to form a "raft")
Box zither (strings suspended over a box)
- Autoharp

Lutes

plucked
- guitar
- mandolin

bowed
- violin

Harps

AEROPHONES

"Free"

Bull-roarer

Whistle

Single
Multiple (many tubes tied together)
- panpipes

Flute

Simple Tube
Notched (with special mouthpiece)
Transverse (held sideways to the mouth)

Reeds

Single
- clarinet

Double
- oboe

"Free"
- harmonica

Horns

even blown (a player can blow against a wooden or metal bar to set it into vibration). An idiophone can be made out of dried plant material, wood, metal, or ceramic (clay).

MEMBRANOPHONES

Membranophones are those instruments that employ a vibrating membrane to create sound. Most common in this group are all types of drums. This membrane in the years before 1900 was most commonly made of animal skin, although it could also be made of bark or other vegetable matter. Today many drums feature plastic membranes, or heads. Membranophones can be struck or rubbed (work by friction).

Von Hornbostel and Sachs noted a special category of membranophones, which they called *singing membranophones*. The most common example today is the kazoo. A player hums into one end of a tube. A membrane of animal skin, vegetable matter, or paper is placed inside of the tube. When the player sings into the tube, the membrane is set into vibration, altering the player's voice. The kazoo that we know today has its roots in African, Greek, and American Indian masks, many of which featured membranes set into the mouthpiece in order to alter the singer's voice.

Above: Drummers Yoruba tribe, Nigeria Africa

Left: Griot playing the Kora (Harp) Bamana tribe, Mali, Africa

PHOTO COURTESY: Natl. Museum of African Art, Smithsonian Institution

CHORDOPHONES

Chordophones feature vibrating strings. The strings are set into vibration or motion by being plucked (as on a guitar), bowed (as on a violin), or struck (as on a piano), to name just three techniques. There are three basic types of chordophones: zithers, harps, and lutes.

Let's take three modern instruments as examples to show the difference between these categories. An *autoharp* is a good example of a zither. On the autoharp, the strings are stretched from one end of the instrument to the other. The body of the instrument serves as a *resonator*; in other words, it amplifies, or makes louder, the sound of the strings.

A good modern example of a lute is the *guitar*. A separate neck is attached to the body of the instrument. This neck serves to stretch the strings, so that they are tight enough to sound at the correct pitch. As on the zither, the strings are parallel to the body of the instrument. Other examples of lutes are mandolins, violins, the Indian *sitar*, and the Japanese *biwa*.

A variant of the lute is the *lyre*. Instead of a neck, a yoke is attached to the top of the body. The strings still run right above the body of the instrument. The lyre was a popular instrument about 2,500 to 5,000 years ago among the ancient Greeks and Egyptians.

Our last type of chordophone is the *harp*. Imagine a modern concert harp, like one you may have seen in a symphony orchestra. The strings run at a right angle to the body of the instrument. Ancient harps have a simple body with a handle or necklike extension. The strings run through the handle down into the body of the instrument.

AEROPHONES

Sachs's and von Hornbostel's fourth category is the *aerophones*. Vibrating air creates the sound. There are four types of aerophones: "free" aerophones; edge instruments, or flutes; reed pipes; and trumpets.

One of the most ancient musical instruments is a good example of a free aerophone. It is known today as the *bull-roarer*. You may have made an instrument like this in an elementary school class. A bull-roarer consists of a piece of wood, ceramic, or other material, usually shaped like a fish. It is attached to a piece of twine, and spun above the player's head. The resulting sound is something like the moaning of the wind. To many ancient cultures, this represented the voice of a deity, or god. This instrument is called a free aerophone because the air that surrounds the bull-roarer is set into vibration by the instrument, creating the sound. Unlike other wind instruments, the air is not contained by the instrument; it is free.

Edge instruments, or flutes, are very ancient. The simplest flute is made from the cane or stem of a bamboo plant (or any other plant with a hollow stem). The player simply blows into one end, against the edge of the stem. The edge of the stem actually breaks up the air that the player is blowing into many separate pulses. These pulses then set the air inside the stem into vibration, creating a sound. The longer or wider the stem, the deeper or lower the sound. On the *recorder*, a mouthpiece is added to the end of the tube, with a built-in edge. This edge acts to break the air into pulsations.

Some flutes have a mouth hole on the side of the instrument. This is true of the modern concert flute. This type of flute is called a *transverse* flute, because it is held sideways or at a right angle to the player's mouth. Again, the mouthpiece serves to direct the player's breath against a sharp edge, which breaks the air into pulsations.

The biggest "flute" you may have seen is a pipe organ. Here bellows replace the human lungs to drive air into the large pipes. At the bottom of an organ pipe you may have noticed a notched indentation. This is like the mouthpiece of a flute; the air is directed by the notched hole against a sharp edge, creating separate pulses that set the air inside the organ pipe into motion. This vibrating air creates the sound that we hear.

Algoza (bamboo trumpet) Ahir tribe, India
PHOTO COURTESY: Roderic Knight

Have you ever held a blade of grass between your fingers, cupped your hands, and then held the grass blade against your lips and blown? You've created a simple reed instrument. The grass blade is a reed, which is set into motion or vibration by the force of your breath. Your cupped hands create a resonator to amplify, or make louder, the sound of the vibrating reed.

Aerophones with reeds can be divided into three categories: *single-reed* instruments (like a clarinet), *double-reed* instruments (like an oboe), and *free-reed* instruments (like a harmonica). In a single-reed instrument, the reed beats against the edge of a mouth-piece. If you look closely at a clarinet mouthpiece, you'll notice there is a tiny space between the reed and the edge of the wood. When this space is open, air can rush through into the body of the clarinet; when it is closed (when the reed presses down against the mouthpiece), no air is allowed into the clarinet's body. The reed acts like a swinging door, rapidly opening and closing this tiny hole. Instead of a steady stream of air rushing through the clarinet, you get small "chunks" of air (or pulsations), which create the vibrations in what is called the air column (the body of air) inside the instrument.

Bassoon reed (double reed), oboe reed (double reed), clarinet reed (single reed)
COURTESY: LaVoz Corporation

Look closely at an oboe reed. The reed on this instrument is called a double reed because it actually is two reeds bonded together. When the player blows against the reeds, each reed beats against the other. Again, the tiny space between the reeds or air hole is either blocked (when the reeds touch) or left open (when the reeds separate). This is what creates the pulsation in the air or the sound.

Free-reed instruments feature reeds that do not beat against a mouthpiece or another reed. Instead, the reeds are attached to a frame at one end. When air rushes against the reed, the reed swings back and forth in the frame. The swinging motion of the reed itself creates a disturbance in the air, setting it into vibration. You've probably never seen a harmonica reed, but if you have an old harmonica that you no longer play, take it apart and you'll see many little free reeds.

Finally there are the trumpets, the last type of aerophone. Remember, we're not just referring to the modern concert trumpet but rather to an entire family of instruments, ranging from a simple conch shell to the modern brass instruments. Here the player's lips vibrate or move rapidly, causing the air to pulse.

Have you ever blown into the end of an empty soda bottle? You hold your lips up against the end of the bottle (which in a musical instrument would be called a mouthpiece). Your lips touch the bottle. You may have noticed a kind of ticklish feeling around your mouth. You may not be aware of it, but your lips are actually vibrating or moving very rapidly. The vibration of your lips is amplified or made stronger by the end of the bottle, which transmits or carries this vibration to the entire surface of the bottle. This sets the air inside the bottle into vibration, which creates the sounds that you hear.

Ancient humans performed the same trick by blowing into the end of a seashell. Again, the lips vibrated, setting the shell into vibration, which sets the air into vibration. This same principle applies to modern trumpets.

ELECTROPHONES

Sachs's and von Hornbostel's system is very handy because it takes into account everything from the simplest to the most complex instruments. However, there have been some recent inventions that don't fit into these categories. To remedy this problem, Sachs added a fifth category, *electrophones*, to include electronic instruments. These instruments produce sound through electronic synthesis; in other words, there are no moving parts that vibrate to create the instrument's sound. Rather, the sound is created by electronic means. The synthesizer is a good example.

Human Beings: The First Musical Instruments?

The human body could be described as the prototype (or model) of all musical instruments. When you think about it, all musical sounds are produced either by vibrating air or a vibrating membrane (solid). The human body contains both basic music producers.

The system of lungs, throat, vocal chords, and mouth forms a musical wind instrument. The lungs supply the air that is driven up through the hollow tube of the throat. The vocal chords, a collection of thin membranes, are set into vibration by the rush of air. The throat and mouth then serve to *resonate* the sound, or to make it louder.

The different vocal pitches are produced in two ways: either by stretching or relaxing the vocal chords or by changing the shape of the mouth cavity. If you think of the vocal chords as being similar to the strings on a guitar, as the vocal chords are tightened (or stretched), the pitch that they produce is raised. Stretching the vocal chords makes their vibrating length shorter, raising the pitch. As the vocal chords are loosened (or relaxed), the tone is dropped. Women's voices are, generally speaking, higher than men's because the length of their vocal chords, at a relaxed position, is shorter. The shorter the length, the higher the pitch.

Try this simple experiment: Hold a rubber band between your fingers and strum on it. Listen to the pitch that you hear. Now pull your fingers apart so that the rubber band is stretched. Is the second pitch that you hear higher or lower than the first pitch? Relax your fingers a little bit so the rubber band is only stretched halfway. What do you hear now?

The sound that the vocal chords make could hardly be heard without some means of *amplification*, or making it louder. The body has a built-in amplifying system, consisting of the throat and the mouth. To understand how this amplification works, we have to understand some basic theories of sound.

Sound, as you may know, moves in waves. Sound waves move through the air at a great speed. Imagine dropping a stone into a puddle. The stone is dropped at just one place. This creates an initial splash, which you can see. As the force of this impact spreads, waves move out across the water in rings. Each ring pushes against its neighbor, spreading the force of the impact to the edge of the puddle.

Sound waves work in a similar way. When you yell, the sound comes out of your mouth in the form of energy or force. This force disturbs the air. A wave is formed, which actually sets the molecules of air into *vibration* or motion. This vibration spreads in waves, pushing out from the initial source of the sound, your mouth. As the energy travels through the air, it loses some of its force. The force is absorbed by the air molecules themselves, which have a natural tendency to stay at rest. Eventually, the sound wave lacks enough energy to move any more molecules, and the sound dies out.

In the human body, the vibration of the vocal chords set air into motion in the throat. This vibrating air is forced into the mouth, which serves as a kind of megaphone (or resonating chamber). The result is an amplified, or louder, sound.

Let's take some examples from the world around us, returning for a moment to the rubber band. How loud was the sound of the twanging rubber band? You probably had to hold your ear fairly close to it to hear anything at all. Try holding the stretched rubber band over an empty tin can. The sound should be louder, because the empty can *amplifies* the sound, or makes it louder.

When you talk into a can, is your voice louder or softer? How about when you stand in a drainpipe or an empty tunnel? In all of these examples, your voice should be louder. Why is this so?

The human body is a model for all wind instruments (or *aerophones*), such as flutes and clarinets. But there is another aspect of the body that serves as a model for drums.

The human skin is a large membrane, stretched over a system of bones. When you pat your stomach, you can feel this membrane vibrate or shake. The vibration of the membrane causes a slapping sound. The hollow stomach and bone structure underneath the membrane serves as a resonator to make the sound louder.

Membranophones are instruments that feature vibrating membranes that are either struck by the hand or a stick or, in some cases, rubbed. It's easy to see that the human skin can also be struck or rubbed to make a sound.

The human body is also the model for all strikers, such as drumsticks. For instance, when you stamp your foot on the ground, you hear a sound. You can imagine that your foot is a drumstick (or the striker) and the ground is the head of a drum (or the object being struck). Humans have made simple striking tubes, to replace the human foot, to strike the ground.

Going Beyond the Human Body

The earliest human beings probably relied solely on their bodies for all their needs. If they needed to rip the skin from an animal, they used their flexible hands and strong fingernails. A hand clenched in a fist could serve as a simple hammer. The body was probably also the first musical instrument, serving to create both melody (through the voice) and rhythm (through slapping the body).

How do we determine what is a musical instrument and what is not? If a person finds a natural object and uses it musically, is it a musical instrument? Or does a musical instrument have to be specially made? Klaus Wachsmann describes one group, the island people who live on Tierra del Fuego, below the southern tip of South America, who make musical instruments out of their limited resources:

> They blow into the windpipe of a newly killed duck, or at the death dances they stamp the ground with pairs of long thick poles, or drum upon a rigid rolled-up piece of hide. Their men bellow into the hollow of their hands placed against the earth, knock sticks and branches against the frame of the festival hut for rhythm, or simply beat the floor of the hut with bare fists.

I believe that the duck's throat, the beating sticks, the piece of hide, and the men's hollow hands are all musical instruments, because they are used to make music.

As we have already seen, it's impossible to determine when the first musical instruments were made. But it is natural to assume that the first instruments were modeled after the body, and used the body in some way, either to resonate the sound, or to supply the necessary force or energy to create the sound. Let's look at some simple examples.

Mouth Bow
Sierra Leone, Africa
PHOTO COURTESY: Roderic Knight

The Mouthbow

One of the most widespread musical instruments in the world is the *mouthbow*. The mouthbow can be made out of many different materials. A tree or plant limb that will bend without breaking serves to stretch a single string, made of either vegetable material (cord) or, more recently, metal. One end of the bow is held up against the edge of the mouth. The player then plucks the string. Although some mouthbows resemble hunting bows, most musicologists now believe that these two examples of human technology are unrelated.

In this instrument, the mouth serves two important functions. One, it makes the sound louder. It is acting as a resonator. Two, it can change the sound that is heard. By changing the shape of the mouth, by moving the jaw up and down, stretching the cheeks, or changing the shape of the opening between the lips, the player actually can produce different tones. How does this work?

When you pluck a string, you hear only one note, the primary tone created by the full vibrating length of the string. However, the vibration of a string is not simple. Imagine again our sound waves. When you strike a string, one wave moves out across the entire length of the string. It then reaches the end of the string, where it bounces back in the other direction. This creates a more complicated vibrating pattern. Imagine now that you are striking the string many times, in rapid succession. The pattern of waves becomes more complicated still.

The result is a very complex pattern of waves, each differing in length. The mouthbow player is able to use this to his advantage. The primary note or tone is always strongest, no matter how much the player changes the shape of his mouth. It is always heard. However, the smaller patterns of waves, called *overtones*, can also be heard, if the shape of the mouth is right.

Air inside a chamber or resonator vibrates or moves back and forth at a fixed speed, depending on the size and shape of the chamber. The air inside your mouth is vibrating at a certain speed whenever you speak. If the player can match the speed of the vibrating air with the speed of the vibrations of one of the string's overtones, the sound of the overtone will suddenly be heard very distinctly. To change the speed of the vibrating air, the player need only alter the size of the cavity inside his mouth.

You don't need to understand the theory of overtones to use them in making music. Early humans didn't discover overtones and then create the mouthbow to take advantage of them. It's more likely that the ability to create overtones was discovered accidentally by early musicians while they were playing the mouth-bow.

Stamped Instruments

An entire family of musical instruments is based on the simple idea that when you stamp your foot, it makes a noise. You can't help but notice this when you walk through a cave, or participate in an energetic dance. The feet are natural percussion instruments; it's pretty hard to miss the beat when the sound of 10 or 12 dancers stamping the ground is heard.

Stamped instruments work on this same idea. For instance, if you put a board under your feet, the resulting sound is louder and clear, simply because the smooth surface of the board vibrates more freely than the muddy earth. If you dig a hole under the board, it vibrates even more freely, because none of its vibrations is absorbed by the earth underneath it. The air in the hole also vibrates, further amplifying the sound.

I've just described what musicologists call a *stamping pit*, and it's a common musical instrument found throughout the world. In some cultures, the hole in the earth that is used to make the stamping pit has special meaning. The voice of the earth is believed to be heard through the sound of the stamping pit. For this reason, the musical instrument has both a practical use and a religious meaning.

Complementing the stamped musical instruments are the stampers. These instruments in a sense replace the feet. Human beings can only stamp on their ground for so long, before their feet become tired and red. However, you can stamp a stick on the ground for as long as your arms hold out. Most common are the stamping tubes, hollow limbs of bamboo plants, which are beat either on the bare ground or on special mats. Stamping tubes make a louder and clearer sound than a stamped human foot.

Stamped instruments are generally played by women. For many women, playing these instruments as part of a dance or special ritual may be the only time that they are allowed to play a musical instrument.

The Slit-Drum

Another common musical instrument is the *slit-drum*. In its simplest form, a slit-drum is simply a tree trunk cut into a section and hollowed out through a narrow opening, or slit. Curt Sachs describes a slit-drum found among the Uitoto Indians of Colombia, South America:

> [The Indians] fell a large tree, hollow out a long groove in the side and paint the whole implement; at one end they decorate it with a woman's head and at the other end with an alligator as a water symbol. A pit is dug in the ground and covered with planks, some logs are placed at either end of them, and the hollowed tree is laid upon the logs so it does not rest on the planks. While the women dance around the pit, the men stand in the groove of the tree trunk, stamping and teetering, and the elastic trunk strikes rhythmically against the planks.

Gigantic slit-drums consisting of an entire tree trunk have been made; they are often kept in special huts that serve not only to protect the instrument from getting wet, but are also holy places because they house the sacred drum. Smaller slit-drums are more common, and can either be stamped or beaten with a stick or with the hands.

Slit gongs from Zaire, Africa.
PHOTOGRAPH: Eliot Elisofon
COURTESY: Natl. Mus of African Art, Smithsonian Institution

What are the Oldest Musical Instruments?

It would be interesting to know which musical instruments were developed first, and where they were first developed. This question might seem to be simple; however, it probably is one that will never be answered.

Most musical instruments are made out of perishable materials— wood decays and ceramics break. Archaeological expeditions have turned up some early stone instruments, but only in widely scattered regions. Documents written on some form of paper, if they ever existed, have decayed by this time. Only paintings on stone or some other imperishable material have survived; only a very few show music being performed.

It is possible to look at the musical instruments that many cultures play today and try to decide which are the oldest. In fact, Curt Sachs did make an outline of the history of musical instruments based on a few simple ideas. These include:

1. The most widespread instruments should also be the oldest.

Why would this be so? Well, if you consider that certain musical instruments are found in almost all tribal cultures throughout the world, this would seem to indicate that these instruments are fairly old. If the musical bow, for example, were first developed in Africa, it would presumably take many years for it to travel from culture to culture to reach the Pacific islands, thousands of miles away.

There is, of course, another way to explain the most widespread musical instruments. The musical bow, simply a string (of bamboo or other vegetable material, in its simplest form) stretched between two ends of a stick, is a fairly easy instrument to make. It is possible that African tribes developed this instrument on their own, while Pacific islanders also developed a similar instrument without ever seeing the African version. In other words, each group may have developed each instrument on its own, responding to similar needs with similar results.

Sachs and others think this is highly unlikely. It is remarkable how many similar instruments are found throughout the world. If you believe that each culture developed its own instruments, you are saying that thousands of different tribes throughout the world developed twenty or thirty remarkably similar musical instruments without ever seeing the work performed by each other. When you think about it this way, it does seem incredible.

In any case, if you accept the idea that each instrument was developed by a specific tribe and then spread throughout the world, the instruments that are most widespread should also be the most ancient.

Sach's second idea is based on his first notion:

2. Musical instruments that are spread over a wide area of a specific region are older than those found only in one geographic area.

In order to understand this idea better, let's take an example from modern life. Let's say you're studying music in New York City. You discover one apartment building where everyone plays the kazoo. It's the only building in the entire city where the kazoo is played. On the other hand, you find buildings scattered all through the city where the guitar is played. It is likely in this situation that the guitar was introduced many years ago, thrived in some areas, died out in others, but in any case spread slowly throughout the entire city. The kazoo on the other hand appears to be newly introduced in one building, and the news of its wonderful features has yet to spread beyond that building.

Sachs then offered a third idea:

3. Musical instruments found only in remote areas, such as closed-off valleys or islands, are older than those found in areas that are easy to reach, such as open plains.

This seems to contradict the previous statements. However, what Sachs means is that those areas that have not had much communication with other cultures have tended to preserve older traditions longer.

Think of it this way: One person lives in an apartment with a TV, radio, and telephone. Many friends visit her throughout the year. She is in constant contact with the latest trends. Imagine that at the beginning of the year she's only heard a musical bow. By the end of the year, she might be playing the electric guitar! It's only natural for someone exposed to all types of music to be changed by this exposure, and to experiment with other types of musical instruments. (This is what happened after Europeans discovered many native tribes, or even when one tribe was discovered by a more powerful group. In either case, the local music and musical instruments were supplanted by the more "modern" music.)

Now imagine a person living in a closed-off room. He never hears any music, except the music played by his immediate family. He only knows the musical instruments that they know. This situation is remarkably similar to an island that is difficult to reach, or a tribe that lives in an isolated area. For them, there probably will be little change, except as individuals contribute to the communal traditions.

For this reason, Sachs believed that isolated tribes tended to preserve older musical instruments.

Using these three ideas, along with evidence from archaeological diggings, cave paintings, and documents, Sachs placed certain instruments in certain time periods. Some have argued with his conclusions; others have decided that he was wrong in one or two cases and made adjustments. As far as we're concerned, it is interesting to know that certain instruments are among the oldest on earth. We don't have to be concerned with which particular one came first.

Sachs believed that the idiophones and aerophones came first, toward the end of the Paleolithic period (approximately 10,000 years ago). This would include simple scrapers and rattles among the idiophones and the bull-roarer and holeless flute (in other words, a simple reed or leaf rolled into a tube) among the aerophones.

During the Neolithic period (approximately 8,000 years ago), the first drum (membranophone) comes in, along with simple chordophones (particularly the musical bow). Among the idiophones, the slit drum and stamping tube developed; flutes with holes and shell trumpets represent the aerophone family.

The most recent of the prehistoric periods brought the xylophone (among the idiophones) and the nose flute (among the aerophones).

More developed instruments, such as harps, lyres, and bowed instruments among the chordophones and reed instruments among the aerophones, are placed by Sachs in the period of early civilization, about 5,000 to 7,000 years ago.

Musical Instrument Making

When it comes to making musical instruments, a lot depends on the natural environment of the culture and the technological know-how that the culture possesses. A society based in a hot, swampy region will probably make very few musical instruments out of stone; plant material will be readily available, and is lighter and easier to work with. Cultures that develop new technologies, including the ability to make ceramics, or to smelt metals, or to synthesize music electronically, will obviously develop different musical instruments.

Musicologist Theodore C. Grame has written about how one plant, bamboo, has had an enormous impact on musical instrument making. Bamboo, a grass plant that is distributed through much

Gourd shakers
Baule tribe, Ivory Coast, Africa
PHOTO COURTESY: Natl. Museum of African Art, Smithsonian Institution

of the world, is a fast-growing and hardy plant. Wherever it has been found, it has been used to make musical instruments. In fact, the bamboo cane is almost a natural flute; when it is cut between two nodes, the cane is perfectly straight and cylindrical (shaped like a pipe or cylinder). Finger holes can be very easily burned into the surface of the bamboo. Within minutes, a flute is made that will last for many years.

Bamboo has another quality that makes it ideal for many stringed instruments. The bamboo cane is made up of many individual fibers, which can be carefully lifted up off of the surface of the plant. If a fiber is lifted up, without removing either end from the bamboo stalk, and a stick is placed under either end to hold it up, the result is a simple, single-stringed zither. In West Africa, a number of bamboo stalks of different lengths, each with a single fiber string, are lashed together to form a *raft zither*. In this way, the musician is able to play many different notes.

Bamboo is most associated in Western minds with China, and it is in the East that bamboo has been elevated to a very important place. The Chinese base their entire musical system on a set of bamboo pipes, as a third century B.C. legend would have it. Many cultures have their own myths about bamboo; a well-known New Guinean myth concerns the invention of the bamboo flute. As Grame relates:

> A man went out into the forest to pick breadfruit. He climbed a tree and threw the fruit down to his waiting wife who caught it. At length a large fruit fell onto a dry stalk of bamboo, which was split by the impact. From the fractured bamboo stalk there came a loud snorting and a terrifying buzzing sound. These noises so frightened the wife that she scurried off. The man ran back to the village to spread the good news: at last something had been discovered that would frighten the women!

In many cultures, the sound of the bamboo flute represents a spiritual voice, a power specially held by men in order to control women.

When we talk about the impact of technology, we have to remember that the cultures that we're discussing in this book live in the 20th-century world. Many have abandoned drums made from natural material, such as gourds, for man-made items, such as tin cans. Colin Turnbull, a Western anthropologist who lived among the Pygmies of the Ituri forest, was distressed when he saw them playing trumpets made out of metal drainpipe, rather than wood. One of the Pygmies had the perfect response: "What does it matter what the [trumpet] is made of? This one makes a great sound, and, besides, it does not rot like wood. It is much trouble to make a wooden one, and then it rots away and you have to make another." In the moist forest, wood does not last as long as in drier climates. It makes perfect sense to adopt a better, more modern solution.

Even though the Pygmies have adopted drainpipes in place of their wooden trumpets, old traditions die hard. The wooden trumpets had to be soaked in water before being played. This soaking had a practical purpose: wood often develops cracks when it dries out; if it is soaked, the wood swells and the cracks close. Turnbull observed Pygmies carefully soaking the metal drainpipes in water, and asked one of them why they continued to soak these instruments. After all, there's no need to soak metal instruments since metal doesn't expand and contract like wood. "We know it makes no difference to the sound," a Pygmy replied, "but we do it anyway."

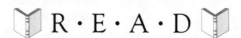

R·E·A·D

Baines, Anthony (ed.), *Musical Instruments through the Ages*. Baltimore: Penguin, 1961.

Collier, James L., *Jugbands and Homemade Music*. New York: Grosset and Dunlap, 1973.

Luttrell, Guy, *The Instruments of Music*. Nashville, TN: Thomas Nelson, 1977.

Weidemann, Charles, *Music in Sticks and Stones*. New York: Exposition Press, 1967.

Sachs, Curt, *The History of Musical Instruments*. New York: Norton, 1940.

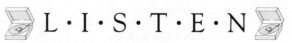

L·I·S·T·E·N

African and Afro-American Drums. Folkways 4502.

The Demonstration Collection of E.M. von Hornbostel. Folkways 4175.

Man's Early Musical Instruments. Folkways 4525.

Pre-Columbian Musical Instruments. Folkways 4177.

The survivors

5

How do ancient cultures, such as the Pygmies in Africa or the Aborigines of Australia, survive today? Are they still living the same lives that they did thousands of years ago? Why is it important that they survive?

Although some of these cultures are more than 40,000 years old, they are changing rapidly as even the most isolated parts of the world are being explored by Western scientists and government officials. Some of these ancient peoples have been relocated to government-run preserves. Although governments want to help these people to survive, the outcome can be a disaster.

There are many different ways in which these ancient peoples have survived. An American Indian who lives in a large city, drives a car to work, and attends a Christian church obviously no longer maintains his or her ancient traditions. This is an extreme case. It is more usual for a person to be caught somewhere in the middle, living in a modern world but still associated with the past. How would you describe an Indian who worked as a computer programmer during the week, and then dressed in ancient Indian dress and participated in Indian religious rituals on the weekend?

First, let's look at where these ancient peoples are found today. What do they share in common? How are they different? Then, in order to understand what has happened to these ancient peoples, we will look back to the history of European exploration of the world, which began some 500 years ago. Some of these European explorers had good intentions; others were merely searching for wealth, and didn't care how they got it. But all had a great impact on the original inhabitants of the lands that they discovered. What have governments done to help these peoples survive? Do these government programs really help them, or are they harmful? Finally, how has contact with Europeans and other cultures changed the music of these ancient peoples?

The World of the Ancient

If we look at a map of the world, we can see certain areas where ancient peoples survive. We are focusing specifically in this book on four areas: northern Australia (the Aborigines), the Pacific islands (Melanesians and Polynesians), the United States (American Indians), and central Africa (Pygmies). These four areas have different climates; the lay of the land or topography is different; the plants and animals that thrive in each area are different; the peoples themselves have different heritages.

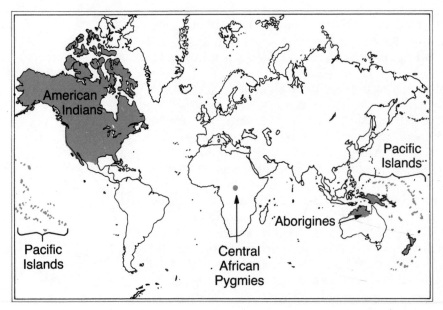

4 Focus Areas in the Book

It is tempting to lump together all primitive or ancient peoples and say, "They're all the same." But think of the difference between a Pygmy who lives in a damp jungle, capturing gigantic elephants through his skills as a hunter, and an Indian living in a desert climate, eating whatever plants he can find and an occasional snake or lizard. The Indian is not very far removed from a great Western civilization, the United States, and is aware of the existence of modern medicine, electricity, the automobile, television, and radio. The Pygmy has little if any contact with these modern conveniences.

When you begin to study these ancient peoples, the differences in their life-styles are truly amazing. The peoples of the Pacific islands live on tiny islands, spread thousands of miles apart, with little or no contact with each other or the modern world. On the other hand, the Indians are in close contact with each other through annual meetings (called powwows), and with the modern world. Some of these ancient peoples are nomadic; they travel freely from place to place, never establishing permanent homes or organized governments. Others have elaborate systems of homes, villages, and "nations," with governing councils and strict rules for how a person can act in society.

You would expect these different peoples to have very different attitudes toward music. The nomadic peoples generally don't have as many musical instruments as the more settled tribes; after all, since they're constantly on the move, they can't have a lot of luggage. Forest people, surrounded by lush leafy plants, tend to make musical instruments out of branches and leaves. Peoples living in the plains use the most abundant resource they have to make musical instruments and tools: the abundant, clayey soil that serves as the raw material for pottery.

Different peoples have different needs for songs and dances. Desert peoples and farmers who depend on their crops for food have developed elaborate rain dances and songs; without rain, they cannot survive. Hunters develop dances and songs to influence the behavior of animals; fishermen create songs for rowing boats. It would be foolish for a Plains Indian to sing a boat-rowing song, particularly since his primary means of transportation is the horse! Societies that separate their young from the older members of the tribe often have initiation ceremonies when a young boy or girl reaches a certain age, anywhere from 7 to 12 years old. These ceremonies draw the line between the carefree years of youth and the responsibilities of being a full member of society. Many include elaborate songs and dance. There will be many more examples in the following chapters.

Among these ancient peoples, music plays a very important role in all aspects of society. As the need for different types of music arises, there is always someone ready to create new types of songs. Young American Indians, anxious to preserve their tribal heritage but influenced by rock 'n' roll, have formed their own rock bands, writing songs with Indian lyrics concerned with Indian topics. They include Indian instruments along with the electric guitars. In a way, this is just the latest adaptation of an ancient music to a changing world.

The Impact of European Exploration on Native Cultures

Beginning in the late 1400's, Europeans rediscovered many peoples of the Earth who had been wholly unknown since the days of the Egyptian, Greek, and Roman Empires. European shipbuilding and navigational skills improved rapidly from the 14th to the 16th centuries; with these skills came the ability to travel to parts of the world that had been previously unexplored. Although long known in myths, these peoples of central and southern Africa, the Pacific islands, and North and South America were seen for the first time by these early European explorers.

The Europeans brought with them only a limited understanding of the world outside of their homelands. They had experienced only one form of government, one culture, one way of raising children and obeying laws, one form of art and music. The native music and art that the Europeans discovered appeared strange to them, because they were raised with entirely different values concerning melody, rhythm, and harmony in music, or color and perspective in art. It was only natural that, since the Europeans felt that their culture was the best in the world, they would try to give to the newly discovered "primitive peoples" the benefits of European civilization.

Many of the European explorers were impressed by the native cultures that they discovered. Most wanted to help these people live a better life. From the European point of view, the natives would be foolish to cling to their old beliefs when they could benefit from the many advantages that the Europeans could bring. The Europeans did not feel that they were robbing the local population of their land and freedom, but rather were bringing them the benefits of European government, money, and religion. The end results varied; in some cases, the Europeans and natives peacefully coexisted; in others, the Europeans took advantage of their superior force (both in manpower and in more developed weaponry) to enslave the natives; in the worst cases, mass murder of natives was allowed in the name of European rule.

The conquest of native cultures began in the 1500's, but came into full swing in the period from 1600 to 1800. In this time, the American continent (now the home of Canada, the United States, and Mexico) was fought over by Spanish, British, French, and Dutch explorers. Australia was used by the British as a dumping ground for serious criminals, because British jails were too crowded to hold them. Africa was opened to the slave trade, particularly along its Western coast. Thousands of Africans were taken from their homes and sold to slave owners in North America and the Caribbean. The Pacific islands were also being explored, primarily by Dutch and British explorers.

The attitudes of the settlers varied greatly. In the United States, the rights of the Indians simply were not recognized. The settlers quickly drove the Indians farther and farther west. Finally the Indians were put on reservations, usually in undesirable locations where survival would be difficult. In Australia, the colonists took advantage of the fact that the Aborigines did not stay in one place. Although for centuries the Aborigines had traveled freely over vast areas of land, the whites now claimed sole ownership of lands that had always been open and free to all people. Soon the Aborigines were driven out of the most desirable areas and placed on reservations, just as the Indians had been uprooted in North America. Africa was a different story; although European countries established governments that were in charge of large territories or areas, it was impossible to control every tribal culture. Many tribes simply ignored the European governments, while others changed their behavior when they were in contact with the Europeans, while continuing ancient customs in the privacy of their own villages.

You would think with all of the power of the Europeans behind them, the conquerors would have destroyed all ancient cultures. The amazing thing is that these ancient peoples, despite the fact that they were often driven from their homes, continued to maintain their rituals and their music. All of the "ancient" music described in this book is still performed today, even if only by an isolated few. And, because it is recorded on phonograph records and in books, its chances of surviving for many more generations looks good.

Government Programs: Helpful or Harmful?

Today many national governments have worked hard to try to help preserve the ancient cultural groups that live within their borders. Sometimes these programs have helped these people survive, bringing modern medicine, farming techniques, education, and technology to groups who have suffered from disease and famine. In other instances, the price of these modern conveniences has been the loss or violation of ancient tribal customs.

Take, for instance, the Australian Aborigines. They are a people used to moving from place to place. Now that they have been forced to remain in one place, they can no longer follow this traveling or nomadic existence. They will have to abandon their traditional way of gathering food through hunting and scavenging; the songs and rituals that were connected with hunting and gathering will probably be lost.

Sometimes it's difficult for the local government to understand ancient customs. Here's another example from Australia. The Aborigines have a rigid social structure, based on dividing the tribe into two groups. A young boy in one group cannot talk to a young girl in the other group. Schoolteachers often try to encourage these children to talk to each other. These teachers have good intentions, and we can understand why they would try to have all of the children play and learn together. However, from an Aborigine point of view, it is a violation of their most sacred laws for the two groups to mix together.

Many people are trying to be more sensitive to these ancient beliefs when they deal with native cultures. However, government rules are often so strict that it is impossible to allow these people the freedom that they deserve. Some groups, such as Iroquois tribes in New York State, have turned down federal aid, preferring to be a separate "nation" within the United States. Although they are deprived of state money, they can follow their own laws. They don't have to conform to rules developed by white government officials that go against ancient tribal beliefs.

Pygmy hunter with arrow & bow.
Ituri forest, Africa
PHOTO COURTESY: Natl. Museum of African Art,
Smithsonian Institution

Pure Versus Contaminated Cultures

As cultures come into contact with each other, they trade much more than just food or clothing. Religious beliefs, superstitions, ways of raising children or managing the family, as well as many other traits can be spread from culture to culture. Sometimes a conquering tribe will purposely seek to eradicate, or stamp out, the native culture. Why should this be? As long as native beliefs exist, the natives can maintain some independence from their conquerors. Giving up native beliefs is in a sense giving up native identity.

A pure culture is one that has never had any contact with any other group. Although we can imagine a pure culture, in fact there. are probably no examples of such purity. Even the most isolated group of people living on an island never explored by Europeans or other native tribes probably is not pure. Why? First of all, they may have come to this place from another place, even if this occurred thousands of years ago. They may have moved more recently around the islands, meeting other natives and adopting their ways. The spread of remarkably similar musical instruments all across the globe, even among the most isolated people, seems to indicate that at some point in time there was a connection between all peoples.

A contaminated culture is one that has had contact with other cultures, whether they be other natives on an island, or other tribes on a continent, or modern, Western civilizations such as anthropologists, musicologists, Peace Corps workers, or other non-native peoples.

In this era of mass communication, in which television, radio, and movies reach the most remote areas, it is even more difficult to imagine people who have not been exposed to some form of European or Western culture. In fact, there still are peoples, particularly on the Pacific islands, who are being discovered. They have no knowledge of European culture, as far as we can tell. But still, it is impossible to measure the purity of their culture, for they may have relations with other native cultures.

Ancient Music in a Modern World

Although we may not like it, music is always changing, along with the culture in which it exists. We may love the traditional music of the American Indians, for instance, but we cannot stop it from changing as Indians have new experiences in a changing world.

These changes can be both positive and negative. Indians have just as much right to play the electric guitar as other Americans. However, some musicologists are very upset when they hear an Indian play the electric guitar. They're abandoning their ancient musical instruments, these musicologists say, and losing contact with thousands of years of cultural life. This may be true, but it is also true that no musicologist has the right to tell a Native American, Pygmy, or Aborigine what kind of music he or she should play, as these people have a right to enjoy *all* types of music, just as we do.

When a Pygmy in Africa makes a trumpet out of a piece of plastic pipe that he finds on an abandoned construction site, he is using a piece of modern technology to express ancient music. The trumpet may be made of plastic, but the music played on it is the same as the music played on the traditional trumpet made out of wood. When a Pygmy buys a modern brass trumpet in a music store and learns to play jazz in the style of Miles Davis, he is also reacting to modern trends. In this case, he is no longer playing Pygmy music, although he might add the sounds, rhythms, or playing styles of Pygmy music to his interpretation of American jazz.

Many American Indians have adopted the modern bass drum from European marching bands to their music. Musicologists feel that the traditional drums made out of wood or pottery that the Indians played are more interesting and more "authentic" than the modern bass drum. Indians feel that the bass drum has a louder sound, and is more appropriate to the large powwows (or meetings) where many Indian dances are performed today.

Many people feel the ancient musics of the world will disappear. I believe that these ancient traditions have a strength that has been underestimated. Although for many years musicologists have been predicting that folk and tribal musics will disappear, this hasn't happened. Native music continues to survive in new forms, shaped by contact with the modern world.

R·E·A·D

Brain, Robert, *The Last Primitive Peoples*. New York: Crown, 1976.

Breeden, Robert (ed.), *Primitive Worlds: People Lost in Time*. Washington, D.C.: National Geographic, 1973.

Breeden, Robert (ed.), *Vanishing Peoples of the Earth*. Washington, D.C.: National Geographic, 1968.

Cotlow, Lewis, *The Twilight of the Primitive*. New York: Macmillan, 1971.

Pinney, Roy, *Vanishing Tribes*. New York: Crowell, 1968.

6

Music of the Aborigines

The Aborigines are among the oldest peoples of the Earth. They have lived in Australia for at least 40,000 years, maintaining a life-style and culture more or less uninterrupted until the British colonization of the continent began in the late 18th century. When the first colonists arrived, many of them convicts and murderers, they quickly drove the Aborigines from the best land into the deserts and other less desirable areas. Meanwhile, missionaries worked hard to convert the Aborigines to Christian beliefs and European customs. Today the Australian government has provided preserves for the Aborigines, much like Indian reservations in the United States, but the old way of life is quickly disappearing as Aborigines intermarry with other cultures, abandon their religious beliefs, and lose their individual tribal identities.

The word "aborigine" comes from two Latin words, *ab/origine*, (meaning "from the beginning"). The Aborigines, although dark-skinned, are not members of the Negroid race but represent a totally separate group of people, called Australoids. Just as in Africa, where there are many distinct tribes with their own customs, there are several hundred Aborigine groups. In this chapter, we will primarily be discussing the Aborigines of northern Australia, particularly those groups that have settled in Arnhem Land, at the north-central tip of the Australian continent.

Society

The Aborigines are nomadic hunters and food-gatherers. Coastal groups also fish. In the past, before specific homelands were established by the government, the Aborigine tribes moved about freely, sometimes taking on new members as they moved, or losing old ones. Occasionally, two tribes would band together temporarily or even on a permanent basis.

The Aborigines have a very complicated social system, with rules for conduct based not only on tribal ties but also family and clan, class, and cult or religion. Although an Aborigine tribe may be very loosely structured, the rules for proper behavior are not to be ignored. They are closely tied with the order of the universe, established by the spiritual powers that created the Earth. Any tampering with the social order, they believe, could lead to natural disaster and death.

The basic division of Aborigine society is into two halves (called *moieties* by anthropologists). Each tribe is divided into groups of clans, each assigned to one moiety. The clans are subdivided into families, and then into subgroups that can range from four to 16 further divisions. There are strict rules for the moieties; a male child in one moiety cannot marry a female in the same moiety. He must marry someone from the other half. Parents in one moiety have the responsibility for caring for all of the children in that group, not just for their own children. On the other hand, children owe the same respect to all parents in the moiety, not just to their own parents. In fact, the Aborigines make no distinction between biological, or natural, parents and all other adults in the moiety who could be a child's parents; a child will call a group of men "father," and a group of women "mother."

This would be complicated enough if there weren't other divisions that cut across tribe-clan-family, but there are. One of the other divisions is based on class. As a person advances in the tribe, learning the special rituals, songs, and other important aspects of culture, he achieves a new class. Another division is based on cult or knowledge of special rituals. As a person learns secret magic spells to control human behavior or the natural world, he gains in power and status in the tribe.

A simple comparison could be made with a small suburban town in America. The town would be like the tribe, a loosely connected group of people. Within the town, there might be a 10-block neighborhood. Let's divide this neighborhood into two 5-block areas. Each one represents a clan. In each 5-block area, there might be 20 children between the ages of 1 and 10, 40 adults between the ages of 15 and 30, and 10 older adults between the ages of 30 and 45. All children would be considered to be brothers and sisters; all of the 15- to 30-year-old adults would be considered mothers and fathers; all of the remaining adults would be grandparents.

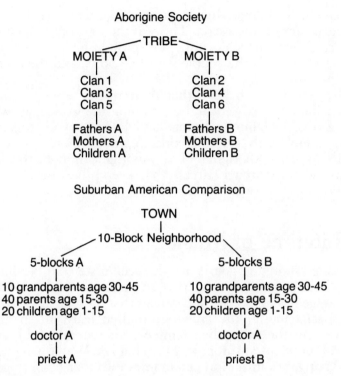

Within each 5-block area, three families might own bigger houses. They would represent a separate class. Also living in each 5-block area is a doctor and a priest; each of these people would represent a different level of cult or scientific/religious knowledge. You can see then that within the general division of suburbia into town-neighborhood-blocks-houses, there are other divisions that cut across these groups, such as owning a bigger house or having special skills.

Aborigine society has one other important division: between men and women. The men serve as hunters, artists, conductors of religious and social rituals, and leaders; women gather food and perform menial tasks. Although we would consider this to be a sexist social order, the Aborigines see it as a natural extension of their belief of a world organized by spiritual forces.

Religion and Ritual

The Aborigines have their own myths or stories about the creation of the Earth. Here's a simplified version of one of those stories: In the days before humans lived on the earth, there were no continents or oceans, forests or deserts. This was the time of "The Dreaming." The Earth was shapeless until the spiritual forces swept across it, creating the land, the people who live on it, and the society that they live in.

The Aborigines believe that their rituals serve as a means of contacting these powers and continuing the work that was begun during The Dreaming. Nature and humans work together; the rituals stimulate the natural world to provide more food and better health for the Aborigine. The Aborigine honors the spiritual/natural worlds through rituals that keep alive the myths of the creation of the world.

A Lifetime of Music

A young Aborigine goes through specific steps to become a full-fledged adult member of the tribe, through a process called *initiation*. Each stage has new songs and dances that must be learned; through this special music, the growing children learn all they need to know about the tribe, their families, the natural world, and basic skills of survival. Anthropologist Richard A. Waterman has divided the Aborigine's initiation ceremonies into four basic stages:

1. Childhood
2. Puberty
3. Bachelorhood
4. Old Age

These initiation rites differ for boys and girls; both girls and boys participate in the first stage, but only the boys pass fully through the last three. After initiation from one stage to the next, the young person is ready to take on a new role in the tribe, with increased knowledge of tribal customs (such as song and dance) and increased ability to carry out important duties (hunting for the boys, parenting for the girls).

An Aborigine song is different from the songs that are sung in Western cultures. A song can last as little as 30 seconds; most songs are no longer than two minutes. Songs are often grouped together to form cycles; in this way, the Aborigines create longer compositions to accompany special rituals. Also, the melody of the song may consist of only a few notes.

For each life stage, there's a different type of song to be learned. Men and women learn different songs; the men learn more songs than the women, and also the more important songs (the karma songs that relate important past events of the family and tribe, and the magical songs that give the singer the power to cast spells):

STAGE	MALE	FEMALE
Childhood	Children's play	Children's play
Puberty	Karma or family history	Ritual wailing
Bachelorhood	Fun	Gossip/courtship
Old Age	Magical	Magical

Waterman studied the Yirkalla group, located in northeastern Arnhem Land. Infants in this group are raised by young girls, up to the age of about 12 when they are ready to be married. This is Waterman's first stage: childhood. During their childhood, young boys and girls sing songs that teach them how to gather food, recognize the different animals, and understand the natural world. The first stage songs are simple play songs, some of which are made up by the children themselves, while others have been known for thousands of years. Dances that imitate the movements of animals or the methods of digging plants or gathering food are taught to the children. The male children also imitate adult ceremonies, including the important initiation ceremony that they will experience at the age of 6 or 7.

When the children reach the second stage, puberty, the boys and girls are separated. Girls are prepared for a life of growing food and parenting children; boys begin their journey toward more specialized knowledge of tribal customs, including the talents necessary for hunting, warfare, and, for a special few, composing and performing music or casting spells.

For the boys, puberty is introduced by a special initiation ceremony. Initiation serves an important purpose: to introduce the young boys to songs that relate his family history. Remember, a boy's family in an Aborigine tribe includes more than just his biological parents. The songs are sung to the boy while his body is painted in special designs that represent the achievements of family and tribe. These songs are called karma songs, and they are sacred to the family.

The initiation ritual precedes the circumcision of the young man, which ends his childhood and makes him a full, adult member of the clan. The circumcision ceremony includes special music and

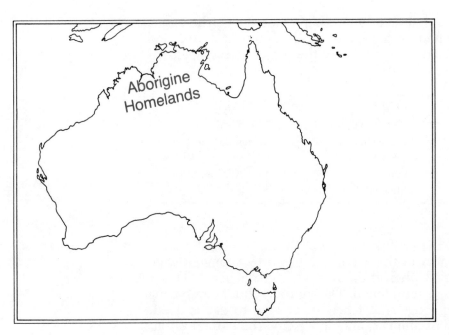

Location of Aborigine Homelands

dance, intended to protect the boy from evil spirits. Waterman describes the song as including hisses, grunts, and screams, and the dance movements as fierce and warlike. The dance ends as the warriors surround the boy, shouting loudly, and the circumcision is performed.

Young girls have their own puberty rites, to prepare them for their roles as parents and food growers. At this stage, the women learn a special kind of song that is only sung by them. These songs have been described as a kind of wailing or crying. The women sing in an intense, strained voice, a tone that starts on a high note and drops through the octaves. This wailing is used to express both great grief and great happiness. The wailing song usually has the same words as karma songs of the same family line.

After circumcision, the boy is removed from the tribe and lives with a group of bachelors. This is the third stage of a young man's initiation, called bachelorhood by Waterman. The bachelors teach the young man songs that have no ritual meaning. Many of these songs are simply fun to sing. Other songs teach the young boy which plants can be safely eaten, which animals to avoid, how safely to hunt, and how to prepare for the different seasons. Songs of fun and entertainment belong to the bachelors and are only sung by them (young women have courtship songs and songs of gossip). During this stage, the young man is taught how to play the most important Aborigine musical instrument, the didjeridu, a wooden trumpet that will be described in greater detail later in the chapter.

The fourth level of maturity is reached after the bachelors marry and reach old age. Age is sacred to the Aborigines, because the older men are thought to be in closer contact with the spiritual world. The songs are learned only by the oldest members of the tribe, and are kept secret because of their great power. They concern the deepest rituals, used only in times of great emergency, and are performed in isolated places. These songs can have either good powers, to promote the growth of food, or bad powers, to put a spell on someone, causing disease or death.

The Aborigines believe that all songs come from the spiritual world. Individual singers do not take credit for composing the songs that they sing. Most songs are communicated to the singer through dreams or when the singer/composer is in a trance-like state. Their source is the world of the spirits. All songs are equally old and sacred; the songs that have been learned more recently, they believe, simply had not been revealed to the tribe as early as other songs that have been known for many years. Aborigines hear music in many everyday sounds; a baby's first whimpers are often used as the basis for a song. The baby's "singing" has its source, the Aborigines believe, in the spiritual world.

Unlike many other cultures, the Aborigines have no work songs. This has been explained by the fact that the Aborigines lead a nomadic life of hunting and gathering; however, other nomadic peoples, such as the Pygmies, do have work songs. It may be because women perform most of the work in Aborigine culture, and few women are encouraged to sing, that work songs have not developed. Since all songs come from the spiritual world, it would be inappropriate to compose songs to accompany work.

In Arnhem Land, a special class of professional singers has developed among the Aborigines. These singers compose topical songs, about everyday events in the life of the tribe, and "dream" songs, relating visions that the singer has had while sleeping. Unlike other Aborigine songs, these songs are recognized as original compositions of the professional singers, and each individual singer has his own repertory, or group of songs, that he sings. The songman also teaches dances to accompany the new songs. Because the songmen are constantly composing new songs, there is a larger group of songs sung in Arnhem Land than in other regions.

Vocal Style and Musical Instruments

The Aborigines have few musical instruments besides clapping sticks, their own bodies, and the wooden trumpet, or didjeridu. Most of the music is sung by a soloist or a group of vocalists. Most Aborigine songs are accompanied by the didjeridu, playing a single note (or drone), and the rhythm sticks. It is the interplay between these parts that creates the rich sound of their music.

The Aborigines have developed a unique vocal style, including the ability to alter the singing voice for different types of songs (called "polyvocality"). The vocal style includes a wide vibrato (called "shaky voice" by the Aborigines), to create a quavering sound. Vocalists also will add many nonvocal sounds to their songs, including hisses, grunts, and shouts. Some Aborigines have developed the ability to sing without interrupting their songs while breathing (in other words, they can sing while breathing in or breathing out), and still others manage to sing more than one note at the same time (a technique that requires great control of the vocal chords).

Australian Aborigine in Western dress

The Aborigines play only two types of instruments: struck idiophones and the didjeridu, an aerophone. Other instruments, such as leaf whistles and bull-roarers, are sometimes heard, but are not as important to their music.

Of the idiophones, the Aborigines generally play either sticks or boomerangs that are knocked together. These are the basic percussive instruments that accompany almost all songs. Slit-drums and wooden gongs are also played, as well as a skin-headed drum (a membranophone) that is only found along the northern coast and is probably an import from Melanesia. The human body is perhaps the favorite percussion instrument, and many dances include slapping the behind, thighs, or stomach, while observers of the dance may clap their hands or stamp their feet.

The didjeridu is the best-known Aborigine instrument. It is usually made from a tree branch that has been hollowed out by termites. A mouthpiece may be attached at the narrower end. In northeast Australia, where there is a plentiful bamboo crop, hollow bamboo stems may be used to make the instrument. In this case, the nodes in the stem must be removed so that they don't block the flow of air in the pipe. In modern times, discarded plastic or metal pipes are favored because they are virtually indestructible.

At first glance, you might think this is a simple instrument to play. After all, it only plays one low note. Actually, you would be very wrong. To play the didjeridu, the player buzzes or vibrates his lips against the mouthpiece, and blows lightly. He produces a single low tone. Brief strong bursts of breath can raise the pitch slightly; by tightening the lips, an even higher note can be produced.

But the greatest variation in tones comes from both buzzing the lips and singing at the same time. The vocal sounds create different vibrations in the air column (or body of air) inside the trumpet, producing many different notes. [For a discussion of how this works, review Chapter 2.] The effects range widely, from sweet tones to sounds that imitate wild animal noises.

The didjeridu player never interrupts the tone by breathing. Once the air in the trumpet is set into motion, he is able to breathe through one nostril, while keeping just enough air pressure going through his lips to maintain the sound.

To become a skilled didjeridu player takes years of practice. Young boys do not simply pick up the instrument and play it. They are taught special "mouth sounds" (songs to sing) that help them remember the many complex rhythmic patterns played by the didjeridu to accompany different songs. We tend to think of all primitive people as being naturally musical. Musical techniques are learned by the Aborigines, even if they don't attend a music school.

Melody and Rhythm

There are basically three types of melodies used by the Aborigines:

1. Monotone (single-note) melodies, used for the karma songs
2. Three or four note melodies, used for songs of entertainment or fun
3. Songs with a very wide range (up to two octaves) and many notes (up to 7 scale tones), used for magical sacred songs.

Of course, some groups only have single-note melodies, while others have wider ranges. The single-note melodies are perfectly suited to songs that tell a complicated story, such as the karma songs that relate family history. The melodies are not really confined to one note, because the singer will vary the pitch as he sings, and the accompanist playing the didjeridu will also introduce other notes.

Although there are many different fun songs, they all share the same melody, and some even share the same words. The difference comes in the rhythmic refrain, which will vary from song to song. By using the same melody for many different songs, the Aborigines make it easier for the young men and women to learn them.

The magical songs are the only songs sung without didjeridu accompaniment. They are accompanied only by special rhythm sticks. The melodies usually drop from a very high note to a very low one.

Besides these differences, melodies can vary from being *syllabic* (one syllable or word per note) to *melismatic* (one syllable sung over many notes). As you might expect, the karma songs tend to be syllabic, since the words are of more importance than the music (even though the meaning of many of the words may be lost because they are so ancient). On the other hand, magical songs tend to be melismatic, as the sound may be more important than the words. Some of the lyrics of the magical songs have no exact meaning at all.

There are several different types of rhythms found in Aborigine music. Some songs are sung in a free style; although sticks are clapped together in a specific pattern, the vocalist seems to ignore this beat. Other songs follow a very rigid rhythmic pattern. Musicologist Trevor Jones has described how rhythm can change within a single song. As in our Western music, a single rhythmic pattern might be repeated many times, with no changes in it. Or, the singer might introduce many different patterns, all following the same basic beat. Or different meters or beats could be introduced in a single song; for example, the singer could start singing in $\frac{3}{4}$

time, then change to $\frac{6}{8}$, then to $\frac{13}{4}$, then to $\frac{9}{8}$, and so on. Or some songs might begin with a regular rhythm, only to abandon it halfway through in a section that has no beat at all. These are only a few possibilities.

Aborigine songs use both additive rhythms and divisive rhythms. In additive rhythms, measures of different lengths are simply strung together, so you might have a 5-beat measure, followed by a 9-beat measure, followed by a 13-beat measure, and so on. In divisive rhythms, each measure can be divided into either 2 or 3 basic pulses; $\frac{2}{4}$ time is an example of a 2-pulse meter, while $\frac{3}{4}$ is an example of a 3-pulse meter.

Polyrhythm, or many different rhythms being played at the same time, is also common. The singer may be singing a melody that follows one basic meter, while the didjeridu player follows another meter, and the percussionists follow yet another. Of course, these meters probably will not remain fixed throughout the song.

Finally, Aborigine rhythm is full of syncopation, or notes falling on the unaccented beat (sometimes called the offbeat). This makes their music sound something like American jazz.

Aborigines Today

From the end of the 18th century to today, the Aborigines have been a people under attack. Australia, as you may know, came under the control of the British government in the late 1700's. Because it was so far removed from England, it was used as a dumping ground for the undesirable members of English society, particularly convicted murderers and other criminals. These colonists quickly pushed the Aborigines off the most fertile land, and killed many of them.

It is estimated that at the time when the English arrived, there were close to 300,000 Aborigines living in Australia. Today only one-sixth of that number remain. Some of the Aborigines have intermarried with the whites, adopting white customs and abandoning ancient beliefs. Others have been placed in preserves, areas protected by the government but usually not the best areas to live in.

Despite the many pressures to change, the old way of life, the music, religious beliefs, and social rules have survived among many Aborigines. Although for some 200 years Westerners have predicted that the Aborigine way of life was doomed to disappear, the Aborigines have defied these dire predictions and continue to make some of the world's most beautiful and unusual music.

 R·E·A·D

Abbie, A.A., *The Original Australians*. New York: Elsevier, 1969.

Cotlow, Lewis, *The Twilight of the Primitive*. New York: Macmillan, 1971.

Malm, William P., *Music Cultures of the Pacific, the Near East, and Asia*. Englewood Cliffs, NJ: Prentice-Hall, 1967.

May, Elizabeth (ed.), *Musics of Many Cultures*. Berkeley, CA: University of California, 1980.

Pinney, Roy, *Vanishing Tribes*. New York: Crowell, 1968.

Rau, Margaret, *Red Earth, Blue Sky: The Australian Outback*. New York: Crowell, 1981.

L·I·S·T·E·N

Authentic Australian Aboriginal Songs and Dances. HMV (Australia) OALP 7504–5, 7516 (3 LPs).

Songs of Aboriginal Australia and Torres Straight. Folkways 4102.

Songs of the Western Australian Desert Aborigines. Folkways 4210.

The Bora of Northeast Australia. Folkways 4211.

Tribal Music of Australia. Folkways 4439.

7

Music of the Pacific Islands

When you think of the Pacific islands, what picture comes to mind? Unless you're very well educated in the history of the world's peoples, you probably think of pretty girls wearing grass skirts danc-

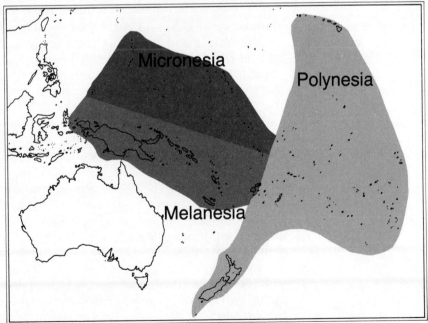

3 Main Divisions of
the Pacific Islands

ing on a sandy beach while the tropical sun sets in the west. This popular stereotype fails to represent even a small portion of the many cultures that are contained in this 750,000-square-mile region that contains somewhere between 7,500 and 10,000 islands (no one has completed an accurate count).

The Pacific islands are usually divided into three main areas, representing three groups of islands.

The first area is Melanesia (from the Greek words *melos* for "black" and *nesos* for "island"). The Melanesian islands are located north and east of Australia, and below the Equator. They include New Guinea, the Solomon Islands and, on the eastern edge of the chain, the Fiji Islands. Micronesia (from the Greek *mikros*, meaning small) is a group of tiny islands situated north and west of the Melanesian group, above the Equator. This group includes the Mariana, Caroline, and Marshall islands. Polynesia (from the Greek *poly*, meaning "many") consists of a group of islands to the east of both Melanesia and Micronesia. The Polynesian group is often described as a triangle, with the Hawaiian Islands at the northern tip of the triangle, New Zealand at the lower western point, and Easter Island at the eastern point.

Although there is a great deal of variation in all three regions in terms of vegetation, animal life, and climate, in general they all enjoy tropical weather with fairly uniform temperatures around 70 degrees Fahrenheit and moist climates. The sea provides an abundance of fish, and coral reefs (found primarily around islands in Micronesia and Polynesia) support lobsters, shrimp, and other marine life. The islands themselves are rich in bamboo, an ideal plant for making musical instruments and tools. Root crops, such as yams, and fruits, such as coconuts, are found on the edges of the islands. The interiors of larger islands like New Guinea or New Caledonia have dense jungles and high mountains. There are a few native mammals, ranging from bats and rats to flying opossums; all food animals, such as pigs and cattle, had to be brought to the islands.

The Pacific islands are richest in music for dance and rituals. Vocal music is more common than instrumental music. Musical instruments are limited to idiophones (such as stamping tubes), membranophones (drums), and flutes or aerophones (including panpipes and nose flutes). The only native stringed instrument is the mouthbow, but Europeans have imported several stringed instruments that have become popular, particularly in Polynesia, including the guitar, which inspired the ukulele. Polyphony, vocal or instrumental music that features several different melodies that are played at the same time, is a common feature of most of the music found in this area.

This chapter provides a brief introduction to the music of Melanesia and Polynesia. Micronesian music is similar to Polynesian styles, and is less well-known than these two other forms. All of these islands have come into contact with European settlers over the last 500 years; the effect on their culture, society, and general well-being has been great. Throughout the chapter, I will be discussing the native styles that have been recorded by musicologists and travelers over the last century; at the end of the chapter, I will discuss how change has come to the Pacific islands.

Melanesia

The Melanesian islands take their name from their dark-skinned inhabitants. These peoples are not of African descent, but are thought to be a special race called Australoid. They came to these islands some 20,000 years ago, perhaps uprooting a group of native Pygmies, who are now found only in the high mountains of New Guinea. Melanesian culture is based on extreme loyalty to the family, which forms the basic unit of society. There is a great deal of warfare among families. Along with warfare, some groups practice

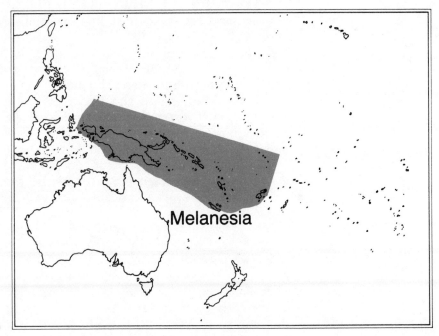

Melanesia Highlands

head-hunting. Melanesians are also famous for their body painting and elaborate tattooing, both of which have ceremonial purposes linked to bringing a young man into the tribe or preparing him for warfare.

New Guinea is not only the largest island among all of the Pacific islands, it is the second largest island in the world, totaling 342,149 square miles. New Guinea is home to a wide variety of peoples, many of whom have yet to be discovered or studied. One anthropologist estimates there are over a thousand different cultural groups on this island. Because two large chains of mountains run down the center of the entire island, travel around the island is difficult, making contact between groups almost nonexistent.

For this reason, small societies, sometimes no bigger than a single family group, have developed, each with its own culture. It is also believed that immigrants came to New Guinea in small groups from about 20,000 years ago until about 4,000 years ago; each group was small enough to preserve its own culture. The isolated areas where many groups settled protected them from too much interference from other societies. Meanwhile, the Pygmies, who date back before the first settlers, were able to survive in valleys in the high mountains, where some 10,000 are still thought to live today.

Melanesians live in small villages; each village is governed by a "Big Man." The Big Man is chosen from among the influential villagers, and acts as a kind of father to all of the members of the culture. The Big Man is said to possess spiritual powers, called *mana*, a power based on the spirits of the dead. Mana can be both good and bad; it can bring fertility to the earth and the family, or it can bring destruction and disease.

The Big Man is also the leader of the warriors. Melanesians participate in two types of battles: short one- or two-day battles, which are preceded by elaborate ceremonies, and more practical raids to take women, land, or heads.

Head-hunting has been described by many Western observers as one of the most savage practices of the Melanesians. Actually, both ceremonial wars and head-hunting raids take only a few lives a year, as compared with European wars that are based on mass killings. Headhunters collect heads as symbols of their defeated enemies; they are often motivated to collect more heads by their wives, who are ashamed to live in the household of a warrior who does not possess enough tokens of his many powers.

One man may take many wives. There is a practical reason for these multiple marriages. The women tend the gardens, and so, from the point of view of survival, a family that has more than one wife will be able to produce more food.

Melanesian music and dance is an important part of their elaborate ceremonies. Some of these ceremonies can take a decade to complete; they center around warfare, initiation (or bringing young men into the society), and mourning for the dead. Dance movements are limited to the lower half of the body, because the dancer often wears a large mask, and needs to have his arms and hands free to support the mask. These masks are meant to represent supernatural or spiritual beings, and the dance movements are exaggerated to emphasize that these are beings from another world. The instrumental accompaniment is often limited to rhythms played on either slit-drums or the popular Melanesian hourglass-shaped drum, which has a single head. The dancers or spectators sing the melody part.

William Malm has described the importance of both the hourglass drum and the songs that it accompanies in the ritual *Hevehe*, a dramatic form that is performed by the Papuan people of New Guinea:

> The hourglass drum and the song it accompanies play a central role in the ceremonial life of New Guinea. . . . Constant musical accompaniment is required for every stage of the cycle [of the Hevehe], including the making of special houses, masks, and costumes beforehand as well as the actual ceremonial events. When this ceremony still flourished, it often took years to complete. . . . The entire cycle might stop for six months if a death occurred in the tribe and the resulting taboo on drumming was not lifted by one of the deceased's relatives. The drum was the symbol of the Hevehe dancer's power. It was relinquished by the dancers only at the final ceremony in which they were symbolically killed and their magnificent masks were destroyed.

Small slit-drums are used for dance accompaniment; larger slit-drums are set into the earth like totem poles, and are owned by the Big Man and are used only on special occasions. A human or animal head is carved at the top of the log from which these large drums are made. Others are horizontal, with an animal or human head carved at one end, and a tail or other decoration carved at the other. The "voices" of the slit-drums (the sounds that are produced when these drums are played) are said to be the voices of ancestral spirits talking to the living.

A single dance may be accompanied by several different melodies that are strung together to accompany the different dance movements. Specific melodies may be associated with specialized dances that are only performed during one stage of a complicated ritual. In one night, seventy or more songs and dances might be performed; some dances have the purpose of moving the dancers from the village to the special dance area, or of moving them around in that area. Other dances are used for special rituals; when a new slit-drum is made, mana is given to it through an elaborate ritual including a circle dance.

Melanesian vocal music reflects the diversity of the peoples who live on these islands. Some vocal music is monophonic, that is, only one melody is sung at a time, either by a solo singer, a group singing in unison, or a group singing in parallel octaves. Call and response is another form that is commonly heard; a soloist sings one part, and then a chorus responds. Polyphony, or several different melodies sung at the same time, is another common style. Songs cover all topics in an average villager's life, from hunting songs to love songs, from songs to celebrate birth to those mourning death.

Melanesian songs usually have complex rhythmic accompaniments. J. W. Layard has described one dance song performed by the Malekula society in the New Hebrides. It includes six different rhythms; the dancers dance to one beat, while vocalists sing in a different rhythm. Meanwhile, four sets of drummers play four different rhythms on slit-drums. This polyrhythm is typical of Melanesian dance music.

The Melanesian people have developed the largest array of musical instruments of any group in the Pacific island chain. However, only a portion of these instruments are played in any one culture. Bamboo is widespread, particularly in New Guinea, and is an ideal material to make all types of instruments. The Melanesian Jew's harp is made from a small section of a bamboo stem. A tongue, or lamella, is cut out of one surface of the bamboo. On many instruments, a string is attached to the tongue; when it's pulled, the lamella vibrates up and down and makes a sound. The entire instrument is held up against the mouth, which serves both as a resonator (to make the sound louder) and to vary the tone that is produced.

A variety of trumpets and flutes are also made of bamboo. The panpipes are made from a number of bamboo stems of different widths and lengths that are tied together. By blowing into the top of each tube, the player is able to play different tones. A nose flute is simply a long section of bamboo stem. The player inserts one end of the tube into one nostril. While blocking the other nostril with the thumb, the player breathes in and out to make the flute play. A simple bamboo trumpet can be made by cutting off a stem right below a node. The node closes one end of the pipe. A small hole is then cut into the node, which serves as a mouthpiece. The player holds this up to the lips and blows against it, allowing the lips to move rapidly. Trumpets can be used to spread vital information; villagers learn to recognize certain signals quickly.

Completing the family of Melanesian instruments are a collection of idiophones, including shakers, rattles, and rasps (instruments that make a sound through the friction of one piece of bamboo rubbed against another). Bull-roarers, thin bamboo disks that are connected to a cord and spun around above the player's head, are played; their sound represents spiritual voices.

Music plays a key role in holding together the society. Malm describes the Kumaon tribe of New Guinea, in which each family keeps two special flutes. These *koa*, as they are known, represent the two sides of the family, father and mother. When a young man reaches the age when he is ready to be initiated into the tribe, he learns how to play these flutes. These instruments represent more than just a means to make music; they are part of the family's legacy, and they contain the physical and spiritual power of the parents that is passed on to the son.

Polynesia

The small island groups that make up Polynesia were settled only about 3,500 years ago, making them the most recently settled land areas on the face of the earth. These peoples are a mix of Australoid

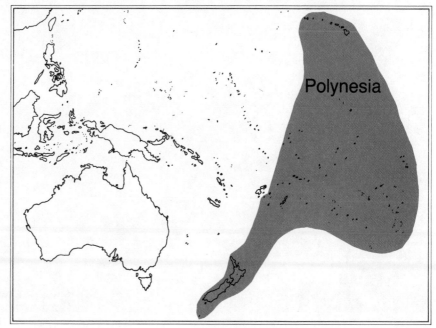

Polynesia

and Mongoloid descents, and are lighter skinned than their Melanesian neighbors. The Fiji Islands, located in the far western end of the chain, are sometimes classed with Melanesia and probably were peopled by Melanesian emigrants.

The islands are volcanic in origin, created by erupting volcanoes that have their bases on the ocean floor. Many of these volcanoes are still active, so the environment on these islands is constantly changing. The volcanoes bring rich soil, promoting abundant food crops. However, the erupting volcanoes can also bring quick destruction to both crops and people. Another problem is the heavy rains of the monsoon season, bringing destruction in the form of floods that kill crops, leading to famine, and also promoting disease.

The Polynesians share many of the same beliefs with their Melanesian neighbors. The concept of mana is also found in Polynesia, and is joined by tabu (sometimes spelled tapu or taboo). Those objects or people that possess mana (or are sacred) are protected by tabu. If a person breaks the tabu code, he or she can be punished by death. Tabus help keep the leaders in society separated from those under them, protect special hunting or gardening grounds, and also protect certain objects used in ritual practices.

Melanesian Hourglass
Drums
PHOTO COURTESY:
Smithsonian Institution,
Natl. Anthropological
Archives.

The social structure in Polynesia is based on a "Big Man" chieftain who runs the entire society, as in Melanesia. However, because the islands are relatively uniform in climate and terrain, it is easier for a single chief to build a larger tribe. Underneath the chief, subchiefs direct the farming that enables the tribe to survive. The chief possesses great mana; he cannot be directly addressed by a member of the tribe. The chief's body also is sacred, with the head the most sacred part and the feet the least sacred part, just as in society the chief (or head) is most sacred, while the lowly farmer (or foot) is least sacred. The chief's barber cannot use his hands to perform everyday tasks, such as feeding himself, for several days after cutting the chief's hair, because he is handling the sacred head. The chief can also make certain objects or people tabu.

Polynesian music can be divided into three major parts: vocal music, music to accompany dance, and instrumental music. These parts overlap; dances will be accompanied by both vocalists and instrumentalists. Let's take a look at each tradition separately.

Vocal music in almost every Polynesian culture is divided into two major categories: recited songs and melodic songs. The recited songs have almost no melody and sometimes no rhythm either; however, they are not merely spoken. Musicologists call this style "heightened speech," because the singer is doing more than just talking. Some of the differences between speech and heightened speech include:

1. A different vocal quality (or sound). The chanting singer may alter his voice to sound more like a spirit or ghost. He may breathe more heavily, use a falsetto voice (singing above his normal vocal range), or produce a raspy or grating sound, to name just a few examples from various traditions.

2. A different vocal "shape." When we speak, the tone or pitch of our voice will vary; in chanted music, the singer approaches a monotone. He will keep very closely to a single note.

The Maori, a society found in New Zealand, use this style both to accompany their traditional dance form, the *haka*, and also for songs relating the history of families within the tribe. These historical songs, called *patere*, give each member of the society a record of the past achievements of his or her family, as well as famous members of the family who are believed to continue to live in the spiritual world. These genealogical songs (songs that relate genealogy or family history) are found throughout Polynesia and are usually sung in this recited or chanted style.

Because the emphasis in these genealogical songs is on the words that they contain, the melody and rhythm tend to be less important

Large slit drums, Melanesia.
PHOTO COURTESY: Smithsonian Institution, Natl. Anthropological Archives

than the lyrics. The melody will center on a single tone, called the *oro* in Maori culture. The singer will then add small decorations to this basic tone, varying the pitch of the music slightly up and down, or changing the timbre or sound that he produces when singing. The rhythm of the song will vary in order to fit in extra words (when needed), or to allow for words that have more syllables than those found in other lines of the lyrics.

Besides genealogical songs, this recited style also can be used for songs that tell tribal history, songs to mourn the dead (and relate their achievements), and songs to recount legends or myths above the spiritual world. In all of these examples, the songs preserve important aspects of the society's culture. Among the Maori, improper performance of words or music of any of these important songs can lead to disaster for the tribe and disease or death for the singer. The Maori even have a word to describe the importance of proper musical performance, *whakaeke*.

The more melodic songs in Polynesian culture generally have a range of three or four notes. These songs concern themselves with all topics of Polynesian life. In Tonga, there are many types of children's songs, including songs to accompany exercise, teach simple counting, and songs simply for entertainment. *Tau 'a' alo*, or work songs, are divided into two groups: songs to accompany everyday tasks, like presenting a slaughtered pig to the village chieftain. There are also songs for lovemaking and courtship found both in Tonga and Hawaii.

There are three basic styles of vocal music: (1) solo; (2) solo with drone; (3) polyphony. Solo vocal music means a single melody is being sung, either by one singer or by a group of singers. In solo music accompanied by a drone, one singer (or group of singers) sings the melody line while another singer (or group) sings a single tone or drone. This is quite common among various Polynesian cultures. Polynesian polyphony, the third vocal style, usually builds on this solo/drone style. Here the melody part is embellished or added to by other singers who sing slight variations of the melody. In different cultures there can be different numbers of embellishing parts, although the usual number falls between four and eight additional parts.

The most elaborate vocal and instrumental music found in Polynesia is used to accompany dances. These dance traditions differ greatly from the Melanesian dance styles. In Polynesia, dances illustrate a poem. The movements of the dancers are designed to accompany the words of the poem that is sung while the dance is taking place. These movements can be quite complicated, and usually involve the upper body (arms, head, neck) rather than the lower body (legs and feet). In fact, some of the dances are performed sitting down, without any lower body movement at all!

Adrienne L. Kaeppler, a musicologist, has made an interesting comparison between the dance music styles of Tonga and Hawaii. In Tonga, Kaeppler found rich polyphony, polyrhythm, and polymovement in native dance. The songs tended to be divided into melody (called *fasi* in Tonga), drone (called *laulalo*), and four decorative or embellishing parts. The dance was accompanied by either struck sticks, rattles, slit-drums, or drums with skin heads, along with hand clapping and the beating of the dancer's feet. Depending on the number of musicians, different rhythms could be created all at once. Meanwhile, groups of dancers would perform slightly different movements, varying arm or head movements slightly, instead of having every dancer performing the same part at the same time.

In Hawaii, Kaeppler found a totally different style. The Hawaiian *hula* is the national dance; we are used to seeing westernized versions of the hula performed in airports, hotels, and nightclubs. Tradition- ally, the hula was a sacred dance, taught by specially trained priests who served under Laka, god of the dance. These priests were employed by the local chieftain, and the dances served to praise the exploits of the chief on earth, and the achievements of the tribe in general.

Hawaiian hula music does not have any polyphony, polyrhythm, or polymovement. Instead of adding parts on top of each other, as is done in Tonga, the Hawaiians instead added more parts to the basic melody, movement, and rhythmic structures. Tongan dance melodies will consist of a small number of notes repeated over and over. In Hawaii, the melody is expanded to include more variations. Similarly, instead of performing the same movements over and over, the Hawaiians have added more variations to the basic movements. Rhythmic variation is created by using different rhythm instruments that produce a wider variety of tones, rather than by playing two, three, four, or more rhythms at the same time. In this sense, Hawaiian music is more like Western classical music; we also embellish or decorate our music by adding on to it, rather than by playing more than one part at the same time.

The musical instrument families found in Polynesia are similar to those found in Melanesia. The nose flute is one of the most widespread instruments. In Tonga, the traditional *upe*, now performed as a lullaby but originally played to wake up a slumbering chieftain or village elder, is usually played on the nose flute. Tongas play four notes on the nose flute, although each instrument usually has six holes. In modern Tonga, the nose flute is played very rarely, and no longer serves as an alarm clock for chieftains. One modern holdover of this ancient tradition can be heard, though; every morning the Tongan radio station begins its broadcast day with the sound of the nose flute.

In Hawaii, nose flutes and whistles (single-note flutes) are used for another purpose. Lovers play these instruments in order to communicate their secret thoughts to each other. The tones that can be produced on each instrument imitate vocal sounds; by listening carefully, the loved one can translate these tones into words.

The Polynesian islands have a rich family of idiophones, such as struck sticks, rattles, gourds, and slit-drums. Most of these are made from the plentiful bamboo plants that are found throughout the region. Hawaii and other regions in the area also have skin-headed drums. Unlike the Melanesian drums, which are shaped like an hourglass, the Hawaiian drum is often made from a hollowed-out section of a tree, and so is cylindrical. One end of the drum is used to form a stand; by carving notches into the log, the drum is given teeth that enable it to grip into the earth, holding the instrument securely upright while the player strikes it.

The Coming of the Europeans

When the Europeans first came to the Pacific islands, they brought with them many changes. Groups of explorers came between the early 1500's and the late 1800's. Most famous was the English Captain James Cook, who made the first maps of the islands, giving them their European names. Later still, Europeans came to the islands to find what they believed would be a more natural life-style; Paul Gauguin, the 19th-century French painter, immortalized his stay in Tahiti in many famous paintings.

Life on the Pacific islands was certainly not carefree before the arrival of the Europeans. Heavy rains and storms often killed all of the crops; tribal wars took their toll on the young men of the tribe. The Europeans brought with them new problems. Possessing more powerful weapons, they could easily overpower the native cultures, in spite of the fact that they were often outnumbered. The Europeans introduced shotguns and other firearms to the natives, which helped to increase the number of deaths in native wars. The explorers also brought alcohol, creating a serious problem of alcoholism leading to many deaths. A more subtle killer was European disease; while Europeans had developed immunity to these diseases because they had been exposed to them for many years, the natives had no such immunity and died in great numbers.

The Europeans quickly acted to end native culture. They wanted to replace native forms of government and social order with their own more "advanced" forms. The purpose, of course, was to take power away from the native chiefs, who could potentially lead uprisings against the Europeans. Missionaries brought from Europe had another mission: to bring religion to the "pagans." This meant replacing native rituals (including music) with Christian rituals imported from Europe.

There is no Pacific island culture, with the possible exception of the Pygmies of New Guinea, that has not been influenced by the Europeans. In Tonga, native polyphony has often been replaced by more conventional European harmony. Church-style harmony, heard in European hymns, now can be heard in all types of native music. Many of the older dances and rituals simply have died out. The Polynesians, generally more peaceful peoples than the Melanesians, have lost more of their cultural heritage than their neighbors, simply because they allowed the Europeans to take over their cultures without offering as much resistance.

This process of cultural change is called *acculturation*. It is most evident in Hawaii, which became the 50th U.S. state in 1959. Even before it was incorporated into the United States, Hawaii had lost a good deal of its native music and dance. Other forms, specifically geared to the entertainment of Europeans and other foreigners, have taken their place. The hula now is danced primarily for entertainment, and no longer has its place as a record of Hawaiian achievements. Guitars and ukuleles now are the primary musical instruments, replacing the traditional nose flutes, drums, and mouthbows. The ukulele is a native invention, but it is based on the European guitar and mandolin, not on any native instruments.

The Pacific islands have not been colonized by as many Europeans as Asians. Asians have come in great numbers since the 1800's, bringing entirely new cultures with them. This too has changed the overall culture on the islands.

Acculturation is not good or bad, it simply is a fact of life. As native cultures come into contact with outside influences, they change. Although we may love the traditional music of the Pacific islands, we cannot turn back the clock to an earlier time when these peoples lived in relative isolation. They will continue to create new music; it may differ greatly from the traditions that were once known, but it still will have a native flavor and, we hope, will preserve some of the native ideas of rhythm and melody.

R · E · A · D

Breeden, Robert (ed.), *Vanishing Peoples of the Earth*. Washington, D.C.: National Geographic, 1968.

Higham, Chris, *The Maoris*. Minneapolis: Lerner, 1983.

Malm, William P., *Music Cultures of the Pacific, the Near East, and Asia*. Englewood Cliffs, NJ: Prentice-Hall, 1967.

McGuire, Edna, *The Maoris of New Zealand*. New York: Macmillan, 1968.

Oliver, Douglas, *The Pacific Islands*. Garden City, NY: Doubleday/Anchor, 1961.

Suggs, Robert, *The Island Civilizations of Polynesia*. New York: Mentor, 1960.

L · I · S · T · E · N

Apparima et Otea. Tahiti Records EL 1017.

Authentic Maori Chants. Kiwi EC-8, EC-9, EC-10 (3 45-rpm records).

The Gauguin Years, Songs and Dance of Tahiti Nonesuch H-72017.

Hawaiian Chant, Hula and Music. Folkways 8750.

Hawaiian Chants, Hula and Love-Dance Songs. Folkways 4271.

Maori Songs of New Zealand. Folkways 4433.

Mele Inoa, Authentic Hawaiian Chants. Poki SP 900B.

Music from South New Guinea. Folkways 4216.

Songs and Games from the Solomon Islands. Folkways 4273.

8

African music

African music is as diverse as African culture. There are hundreds, if not thousands, of different cultural groups in Africa, and each has its own form of music. Although there are some similarities, particularly among the black cultures, there are a wealth of differences. In this chapter, I will discuss some of the basic similarities in African music, while focusing on a unique tradition of central Africa, the Pygmy music of the Ituri Forest.

Africa can be conveniently divided into two main areas: North Africa and sub-Saharan Africa. North Africa, including the enormous Sahara Desert, is made up of various tribal groups. Although there are black peoples living in this region, the Arabs have had the greatest impact on North African music and culture. Arabic music is closer in style to Western music; in fact, about 1,000 years ago, Westerners came into contact with the Arabs, and incorporated many of their ideas about music composition and notation into our music system. In Arabic cultures, musicians tend to be professionals; they have no other job but the performance, preservation, and composition of music. Many musicians serve the important task of preserving famous myths, legends, and histories of a particular culture.

On the other hand, sub-Saharan Africa (all of the land below the southern edge of the great desert) does not have a direct Arabian influence. Most of the tribal groups, with the exception of the Pygmies, are Negroid (members of the black race). When Westerners discuss African music, they are generally referring to these sub-Saharan cultures.

Further divisions could be made in sub-Saharan Africa by geographic area (east central versus west central Africa, coastal versus inland areas, and so on). Beyond these very large divisions, you really have to look at each individual culture as a separate and unique development.

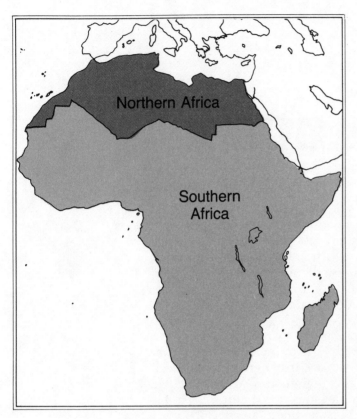

Two Main Divisions of Africa

Most of these societies share a general approach to music: (1) Music performance is communal, not individual. (2) Music plays a role in all parts of life. (3) Music mimics language. (4) "Muddy" tones are preferred over "pure" tones. (5) Polyrhythms are preferred over monorhythms. (6) Music is enjoyed, not analyzed or studied.

Let's take a look at each of these ideas.

Communal Music

Unlike the Arabic cultures of North Africa, all sub-Saharan Africans participate in music making. This does not mean that there are no music specialists. The *griots* of Gambia are specialized musician/performers who sing songs relating the history of their tribes. They accompany themselves on the *kora*, a harp that may originally have come from the North. In fact, these griots are very similar to the Arabian poet/musicians, because they form a separate musical class, are highly trained, and have no other occupation within the tribe.

However, the griot is really an exception to the rule. In most African tribal cultures, music making is shared by all. There may be specialists who take the solo vocal parts, or direct the musical part of a ritual. However, everyone is expected to add a voice to the communal singing.

The call-and-response format of many African songs allows everyone to participate, even those who may not be musically talented. In call-and-response, one line is sung by a soloist (the "call"), which is followed by a line sung by a chorus (the "response"). The call part is taken by a talented singer who can handle a solo part. The response can be sung by everybody; if someone has difficulty carrying the tune, the rest of the chorus can help him or her along.

Even the more talented musicians will generally have other jobs in the tribe besides making music. They will be expected to pitch in with hunting, warfare, religious rites, and other tribal functions. The culture's songs are not considered to be the property of any one musician, as they are in Arabic culture. Songs are learned by all members of the tribe, and are "owned" by everyone. At each new stage of life—whether it be the passage from being a child to a young man, or from a young man to an adult—new songs are learned.

Music Is a Part of All Life

Musicians are not separated from the rest of society; music is also not separated from everyday tasks in life. In the West, we will go to a concert to hear music. Music making is limited to this special occasion, when we listeners can enjoy the performance of professional musicians. In most African cultures, there are no listeners; everyone participates in music making. Music making does not take place only in special places on special occasions; it occurs throughout all social functions.

Depending on the culture, music will accompany everyday tasks involved in agriculture (planting, weeding, pounding grain, harvesting the crops), religion (casting spells, enlisting spiritual aid to ensure better personal health), hunting (invoking the animal spirits to guarantee a successful hunt), building (work songs while constructing either communal or individual dwellings), and on and on. Each culture crafts songs for its individual needs; the Pygmies have many songs concerning elephant hunting, their primary source of meat. Other tribes that do not hunt the elephant have no need for elaborate songs and ceremonies concerning this animal, and so have none.

Music Mimics Language

Many African languages are tonal or pitch languages. In other words, the same word, pronounced with a different inflection or

Xylophone player
Bamana tribe,
Mali, Africa
PHOTOGRAPH: Eliot
Elisofon
PHOTO COURTESY:
Natl. Museum of
African Art,
Smithsonian Institution

pitch, has a different meaning. A smaller number of languages also include other sounds besides speech; the best known are the click languages that utilize the clicking of the tongue as well as more ordinary speech sounds. In this way, music is built into the African languages. Because speech varies in pitch, you can almost hear the beginnings of melodies in the everyday language. Indeed, some musicologists believe music had its beginnings in this way.

Many African cultures have created "talking" musical instruments that mimic or imitate vocal sounds. Talking drums are the best known examples. These are usually slit-drums. A complete tree trunk, or a short section of it, is hollowed out in various thicknesses, so that when it is struck in different spots it produces different tones. The skilled drummer is able to beat patterns that reproduce the pattern of tones heard in everyday language. Originally, these talking instruments were thought to hold the voices of spirits. Spirits were said to talk through the music of the drums. Talking drums were also used to send messages across vast distances.

African trumpets also show this connection between speech and music. A simple trumpet is merely a hollowed out tube that tapers from a wide bell (or end opening) to a small mouthpiece (or simply a hole to blow in). Some Africans speak into the trumpet and use it as a megaphone to amplify their voices. Others hum and blow into the trumpet at the same time; this produces a sound that is neither pure voice nor pure trumpet. Still others play the trumpet without making any extra vocal sound. It is impossible to say if the trumpet was first developed to serve as a megaphone, with its musical capabilities accidentally discovered at some later date, or vice versa. Trumpets are used today to send messages, just as talking drums are, by playing musical phrases (or a collection of tones) that imitate or mimic the pattern of tones heard in spoken phrases.

Muddy Tones Versus Pure Tones

A pure tone is the sound that is produced when you pluck a string, blow into a tube, or strike a xylophone key, without in any way interfering with its natural vibration. Muddy tones are tones that are purposely altered or changed by the musician.

There are many examples of muddy tones in African music. For example, instead of simply blowing into a flute, an African musician will often hum into it. The humming distorts or changes the natural sound of the flute, and can be clearly heard while the musician plays.

One of the most complicated African instruments, called the *mbira* or *sansa* (among other names) and known in this country as the thumb piano, is almost always altered to produce muddy tones. The mbira consists of a series of metal tongues, secured at one end to a block of wood, which are plucked by the fingers of the musician. The length of the tongue determines the pitch that it will produce. When the tongue is plucked, it vibrates, producing a pure sound. On most mbiras, however, musical instrument makers add small pieces of metal or some other material that is wrapped around each tongue. These metal pieces impede or slow down the vibration, and also vibrate themselves, adding a rasping or buzzing sound to the pure tone.

Even African vocal music emphasizes a harsh, grating sound rather than a more relaxed singing style. Many African vocalists come close to shouting, keeping their throats very tense, purposely creating a sharp, raspy sound.

It is difficult for us to understand the African's love of muddy sounds. We take just the opposite approach to music, always seeking to eliminate anything that changes the sound of a musical instrument. But just because the African musician has a different point of view does not mean that he or she fails to understand the "correct" way to play music. It just means that these African musicians are striving to create different types of sounds than we do.

Polyrhythms

Most of African music is highly rhythmic, with complex interlocking drum parts. Instead of playing a single rhythm on a number of drums, each drum part may be independent of the others. In this way, African musicians create polyrhythms or, in other words, pieces of music that feature more than one rhythm being played at the same time. At first, the resulting composition may sound merely like confusing noise to us. But remember, as Westerners we simply are not used to listening to multiple rhythms. An "educated" African audience would have no difficulty listening to and understanding this music.

Music Isn't Analyzed

In Western cultures, we study music just as we study biology, literature, or any other subject. When we analyze or study music, we notate the melody, fit it into a musical key, note its rhythm, look at how the notes flow up and down from low pitches to high, study the harmony, and try to interpret the composer's intentions in creating this work of music.

In traditional African cultures, music is never studied, nor is biology, literature, or any other subject studied in a classroom. There aren't even any classrooms! Music is so much a part of life, with everyone in the tribe understanding and participating in it, that there is no need for someone to come along and explain music to the tribe's members.

Alan Merriam, a Western musicologist who specialized in African music, made an important comment concerning this lack of music theory or ideas about music. He warned Westerners not to dismiss African music just because their music didn't appear to have any rules. In fact, there are complicated rules for African music, just as there are for Western music. However, unlike Western music, in which these rules have been written down, there is no need for Africans to write down musical rules. Everyone who plays music knows the rules. Although Africans can't answer questions about music theory or biology or literature, this does not mean that they have no knowledge about music, the world around them, or their own legends and myths. It simply means that they have no need to separate knowledge from how they act.

The Pygmies

Deep in the jungles of the Ituri rain forest of central Africa lives a group of people who are said to be among the oldest cultures found in the world. Although no one is certain, it is possible that the Pygmies have lived in the same way since the Paleolithic era, some 10,000 to 50,000 years ago.

The Pygmies were given their name by ancient Greek philosophers; *pygmaois* is the Greek word for "cubit," a measure of length that equals approximately 20 inches. Records of the Pygmies

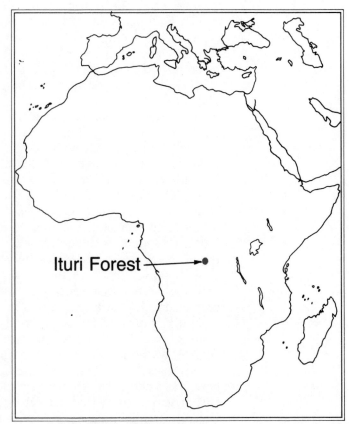

Ituri Forest, home
of the Pygmies

go back to the ancient Egyptians, about 5,000 years ago. One pharoah sent a search party deep into central Africa. They returned with Pygmies who served as musicians and entertainers in the Egyptian court.

The Pygmies are not racially the same as black Africans. They are a separate race, called Pygmoid. However, of the approximately 160,000 Pygmies living today, only about one-sixth still live in the forests and have maintained the Pygmy way of life. The remainder have intermarried with other tribes around them, particularly the Bantu, and have taken up the customs of their neighbors.

Pygmies traditionally have lived in the forest, making temporary homes in the treetops, without any permanent villages. While other African tribes are frightened of the forest—because so many wild animals live in it, and also because it is said to be the home of supernatural, evil spirits—the Pygmies have adapted themselves to forest life. In fact, the forest has protected these people remarkably well, because their neighbors, who are physically bigger and stronger, are too frightened to pursue them into the forest.

The Pygmies are nomadic; they move from place to place. They are hunters, living on elephant meat. How do such small people capture large elephants? They have learned to make effective poisons and have developed skills as hunters. They can move quickly along the forest floor; their small size makes them both fast and difficult for larger animals to see. They use only one weapon on the hunt: poisoned darts. Pygmies can throw a dart a great distance with remarkable accuracy.

The Pygmies' religion is *monotheistic*; instead of believing in a number of spirits, each having limited powers, the Pygmies believe in a single god who has power over all natural events. The elephant is so important to the Pygmies that their god is often described as "the elephant father of the world." There are no priests or a church; religion, like music, is shared equally by all.

Pygmy society is divided by sex. The men are the hunters, while the women are in charge of building the mud-and-leaf huts. Although polygamy, or a man taking many wives, is allowed, it is extremely rare, because it would be difficult for one man to provide enough food for a large family.

The Pygmies probably originally lived outside the forest. However, about 2,000 years ago, the Bantu tribes came to central Africa. With greater size and strength, the Bantu could easily have exterminated the Pygmies. However, the Pygmies were clever enough to adopt the Bantu way of life, when they were in contact with the Bantu, while retreating from their original homelands

Pygmy in front of hut
Ituri forest, Africa
PHOTOGRAPH: Eliot Elisofon
PHOTO COURTESY: Natl. Museum of African Art,
Smithsonian Institution

into the forest. Once in the forest, they developed a mutually beneficial relationship with the Bantu. They provided the Bantu with elephant and other animal meats and skins; in return, the Bantu offered them musical instruments, and other things that the Pygmies had never seen. This relationship continues today.

Over the years, the Pygmies have learned to live with the neighboring Bantu. Along the way, the Pygmies lost their own language; today, they speak four different dialects, all part of the Bantu language family. Pygmies are classified by these four dialects: (1) Ba-Binga; (2) Ba-Ngombe; (3) Ba-Mbuti; (4) Ba-Benzele.

For many years, Pygmy culture was misunderstood by Westerners, because Pygmies were only seen when they were living in Bantu villages. When Pygmies trade with the Bantu, they live temporarily outside the forest in the Bantu village. They practice Bantu rituals, speak the Bantu language, even participate in Bantu music making. However, as soon as they return to the forest, they take up their own traditions again. Because few Westerners actually followed them into the forest, most believed Pygmy culture was the same as Bantu culture. Eventually, a few anthropologists went into the forest, and the result was the surprising discovery of Pygmy culture. Colin Turnbull, a British anthropologist, tells the story of his own introduction to Pygmy society in his book, *The Forest People*.

Vocal Music

Traditional Pygmy music is primarily vocal music. When a group of Pygmies sing together, they use a special ensemble vocal technique called *hocketing*. Let's say a song consists of only a single note or tone. Two singers wish to sing together, but do not want to sing at the same time. So they alternate; the first one sings the note for a short period of time, and then the second singer sings the same note while the first singer rests. This is called a simple hocket; the singers alternate singing the same note.

Now, let's say a group of singers want to sing a song that consists of several notes. Each singer can be assigned a single note. Every time that note occurs in the melody, he or she sings it. In this way, a musical group can be formed that puts only limited demands, in terms of musical ability or training, on each member. This is a more complex form of hocketing.

The Pygmies have developed a kind of solo hocketing. An individual singer makes a leaf whistle that plays only one note. He or she blows on the whistle to play that note. In effect, the whistle is one voice or singer. The singer then alternates blowing on the whistle and singing either the same note or a slightly different pitch. The singer's voice is the second part of the hocket.

When the Pygmies sing, they use several special vocal techniques. The yodel, a quick change from a head voice (breathing centered in the throat and nose) to a chest voice (full breathing coming from the diaphragm or chest), is found in all Pygmy vocal music. By rapidly opening and closing a section of the throat called the *glottis*, the Pygmies create an interrupted or quavering sound. This vocal technique is called a glottal attack. The Pygmies will also interrupt their singing with shouts, grunts, and humming and buzzing sounds, to make a more muddy tone. Trills and tremolos (rapid up and down glides above and below the primary pitch) are another technique found in Pygmy vocal music.

The Structure of Pygmy Songs

Pygmy music is structured around several short sections that are put together to form a song. This is called an *additive structure*, because parts are added together. There may be no overall shape to a song; on different occasions, different parts might be added or dropped. The rhythm of the song is also additive. Rather than an entire song following one rhythmic pulse, the Pygmies will put together measures based on 2-beat pulses followed by measures based on 3-beat pulses. For example, 3 measures in $\frac{2}{4}$ time (march time) might be followed by 2 measures in $\frac{3}{4}$ time (waltz time). Musicologists call a pattern of 3 measures of 2 beats followed by 2 measures of 3 beats *hemiola*. Hemiola is quite common in Pygmy music.

When several rhythmic units are added together in a long string of measures, a horizontal rhythmic structure is formed. Only one beat is occurring at a time, but the rhythmic pulse varies as the measures switch from being based on a 2-beat structure to a 3-beat structure and back again. Vertical rhythmic structures have more than one rhythmic pulse occurring at the same time. For example, if one group of singers were singing a melody consisting of 3 measures based on a 2-beat rhythm, while another group of singers simultaneously were singing 2 measures based on a 3-beat rhythm, the effect would be called vertical hemiola. Both horizontal and vertical hemiola is found in Pygmy music.

Song Subjects

The subjects of Pygmy songs can be divided into three different groups: (1) Hunting and food-gathering songs (particularly songs related to the elephant hunt); (2) Songs for amusement (games, dances, drinking, lovemaking) (3) Songs of the religious societies.

Elephant hunting songs fall into two groups: sacred songs that are sung before and after the hunt, in order to guarantee its success,

Pygmy dancers with drums and bamboo whistles
Ituri Forest, Africa
PHOTOGRAPH: Eliot Elisofon
PHOTO COURTESY: Natl. Museum of African Art, Smithsonian Institution

and social songs sung during the evening following a hunt, to tell the story of the day's adventures. The sacred songs are very important; they must be sung correctly or the success of the hunt will be jeopardized. The social songs are sung by a group of men; one man takes the lead, narrating the exploits of the day, while a group of men sing behind him in the hocketing style. Each member of the chorus sings a single note at the correct time to form the melodic background.

Gathering food is performed by both men and women, because the survival of the tribe depends on full participation of all members in the search for food. Songs are sung while the Pygmies search for food, for amusement, as a means of communicating (it may be difficult to see other members of the tribe as they spread out across the floor of the forest), and as a way of keeping the group working together.

Songs for amusement can be sung by an individual or a group, in a hocketing style or a solo style. As in other African tribes, the Pygmies sing about every subject that affects their lives, including songs to amuse children, songs to accompany games, songs of love and courtship, and songs to accompany everyday tasks.

The Pygmies have two religious societies, the *molimo* for the men and the *elima* for the women. The molimo is actually a sacred trumpet, and is played during several nights of singing and dancing. This festival can last a month or more. Its purpose is to rid the tribe of some evil influence, whether it be sickness, drought, or failure at the hunt. The sound of the trumpet is thought to waken the good spirits in the forest, who will come to the aid of the suffering Pygmies. The trumpet, traditionally made of bamboo, mimics the songs sung by the men around the special molimo fire, and also imitates the wild sounds of the forest's dangerous animals. The molimo is only practiced in a secluded part of the forest, and the women are forbidden to hear the special songs.

A Pygmy described to Colin Turnbull the importance of the molimo festival:

> Normally everything goes well in our world. But at night when we are sleeping, sometimes things go wrong, because we are not awake to stop them. . . . Army ants invade the camp; leopards may come in and steal a hunting dog or even a child. If we were awake these things would not happen. So when something big goes wrong, like illness or bad hunting or death, it must be because the forest is sleeping and not looking after its children. So what do we do? We wake it up. We wake it up by singing to it, and we do this because we want it to awaken happy. . . . When our world is going well then also we sing to the forest because we want it to share our happiness.

Elima is the female's own special festival. It occurs when a young girl reaches puberty. She must be purified and made ready to bear children. The women retreat to a special area, where sacred songs are sung for the girl. The Pygmies fear blood, because it is connected with sickness and death; but they recognize that the bleeding that occurs when a girl reaches puberty is healthy and important to the continuing growth of the tribe. The elima both eliminates the evil associated with blood and celebrates the fertility of the young woman.

Musical Instruments

The Pygmies don't have many musical instruments; because they are always on the move, the Pygmies cannot make heavy instruments, such as the large slit-drums that are played by their neighbors and housed in special, permanent buildings. However, contact with the Bantu has introduced some smaller musical instruments to the Pygmies, including small, portable slit-drums, nose flutes, musical bows, one-string zithers, and modern instruments including bottles, spoons, and even the guitar. The most common instrument is the small leaf whistle. The Pygmies make whistles by rolling a leaf into a small pipe; however, these instruments don't last long in the damp forests. The leaves soon rot, and new whistles have to be made constantly.

The Future

There are two threats to the continued existence of Pygmy culture and music: the intermarriage of Pygmies with their Bantu neighbors and the introduction of new ways of life by Europeans and other outsiders

The Pygmies seem to have survived 2,000 years of living with the Bantu. Although the Pygmies have regular contact with the Bantu and sometimes live in their villages, their culture remains unaffected as long as they can continue to retreat to the forest. The forest has proven to be a remarkable friend to the Pygmies, and they have repaid this friendship through their rituals praising the god of the forest.

The continued contact with Western ideas is more difficult to measure. The life of the forest itself could be threatened as more development of industry and housing comes to central Africa. Also, governments have difficulty controlling individual groups like the Pygmies, who live within their borders. They usually try to destroy the ancient tribal structures, in order to get better control over these peoples.

The Pygmies have managed to survive tens of thousands of years despite being smaller and more vulnerable than most other people. Their love for the natural world and respect for its rhythms is something that we Westerners seem to have lost touch with. For this reason alone, it's important that the Pygmies can continue to survive despite the changing nature of life in the Ituri forest.

R·E·A·D

General

Bebey, Francis, *African Music*. New York: Lawrence Hill, 1975.

Blacking, John, *How Musical Is Man?* Seattle: University of Washington Press, 1972.

Coughlan, R., *Tropical Africa*. New York: Time-Life Books, 1966.

Kebede, Ashenafi, *Roots of Black Music*. Englewood Cliffs, NJ: Prentice-Hall, 1982.

Nettl, Bruno, *Folk and Traditional Music of the Western Continents* (2nd ed). Englewood Cliffs, NJ: Prentice-Hall, 1973.

Nketia, J. H. Kwabena, *The Music of Africa*. New York: Norton, 1974.

Roberts, John Storm, *Black Music of Two Worlds*. New York: Praeger, 1972.

Warren, Fred, and Lee Warren, *The Music of Africa: An Introduction*. Englewood Cliffs, NJ: Prentice-Hall, 1976.

Books About the Pygmies

Bleeker, S., *The Pygmies*. New York: Morrow, 1968.

Shepherd, E., *In a Pygmy Camp*. New York: Lothrop, Lee, and Shepard, 1969.

Turnbull, Colin M., *The Forest People: A Study of the Pygmies of the Congo*. New York: Simon & Schuster/Touchstone Books, 1962.

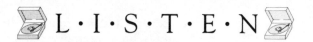

L·I·S·T·E·N

General

The African Mbira. Nonesuch H 72043.

Africa South of the Sahara. Folkways 4503.

Africa: East and West. Institute of Ethnomusicology 6751.

African Musical Instruments. Folkways 8460.

African Story Songs. University of Washington Press UMP-901.

East Africa: Bantu Music. CBS Special Series 9/A-02017.

Folk Music of the Western Congo. Folkways 4427.

Music of Zaire, Vols. 1 and 2. Folkways 4241, 4242.

Songs of the Watusi. Folkways 4428.

The Music of the Dan. UNESCO Collection/Baren Reiter Musicaphon 30 L 2301.

Voices of Africa. Nonesuch H 72026.

Pygmy Music

Music from an Equatorial Microcosm. Folkways 4214.

Music of Equatorial Africa. Folkways 4402.

Music of the Ba-Benzele Pygmies. UNESCO Collection/Baren Reiter Musicaphon 30 L 2303.

The Pygmies of the Ituri Forest, Congo. Folkways 4457.

Music of native Americans

9

At one time, the North American continent was home to more than the three large nations of the United States, Canada and Mexico. In fact, there were thousands of different cultures flourishing here, some peaceful, some warlike, some living in harmony with the natural world and their neighbors, others conquering or being conquered as their power increased or decreased. These were the nations of Native American Indians, not a single culture as you might imagine, but many different peoples, each with a unique culture.

The American Indians have been more thoroughly studied than almost any other peoples on earth, simply because they live in America. Anthropologists can make a short trip to an Indian reservation and study their music, art, and life-style. The music of the Indians has been recorded since the very earliest days of sound recording, in the 1890's, by pioneer musicologists like Frances Densmore. Yet even though there is so much information available about the Indians, the myths and stereotypes about the Indians remain powerful.

We may think that we know a lot about Indians. After all, they live right here in America. But very few of us have probably seen an Indian, unless we live near the Western reservations. What we have seen are countless Westerns on TV and in the movies, but these give a distorted view of what Indian life is really like. Even the name "Indian" is based on a misconception; as you may know,

Columbus sailed from Spain in the late 15th century searching for a new route to India. When he arrived in the New World, he thought he had reached his destination, and so gave the natives the name "Indians," and this name has stuck.

The exploration and eventual settlement of North America by the Europeans had a great impact on Indian life. When the Indians first encountered the white European settlers, some of them happily shared with the settlers their knowledge of the American continent; others fought furiously against the conquerors. With few exceptions, all were overpowered and large numbers were eventually exterminated by the settlers, who believed that the American continent was destined to belong to the white people.

In this chapter, we will examine the rich variety of American Indian culture through one very special aspect of their lives, their music. It is impossible in this limited space to discuss the music of all of the tribes; instead, we will first introduce some of the major tribes and where they live, then examine some general aspects of Indian music and the musical instruments that they play, and finally focus on three representative tribes.

An Introduction to the Tribes

Many geologists believe that, thousands of years ago, the North American continent was attached to Asia by a thin land bridge. Ancient Asian peoples slowly crossed this bridge, and came to populate North America. It is believed that these were the ancestors of the American Indians.

There are approximately a thousand known Indian tribes living from Alaska and the Canadian north to the bottom of South America. Of these, some 100 tribes have been studied in depth by anthropologists. The Indians have 60 different language families, or groups of related languages. The Indians who lived on the American continent are as varied as the continent itself. Anthropologists, such as David P. McAllester, have grouped the North American tribes by the area of the continent where they lived. These groupings include:

1. Woodlands (north and southeastern U.S. and Canada), including the Iroquois
2. Plains (Sioux, Cheyenne)
3. Southwest (Navaho, Apache, Pueblo Indians)
4. Plateau or Great Basin (Paiute)
5. Northwest Coast (Kwakiutl)
6. Arctic (Eskimos)

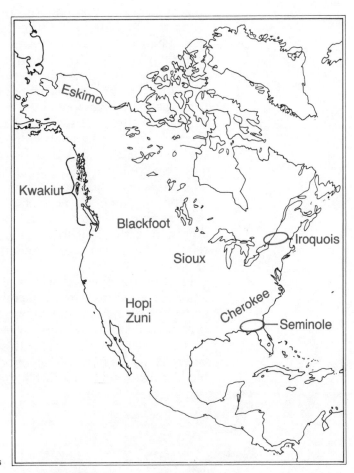

Location of American Indians

The Woodlands Indians of the Eastern coast lived a life centered on villages. In the South, they farmed, while in the North, where woodlands were thicker and farming more difficult, animals were hunted for both food and skins. Everyday, in dance and song, the Woodlanders gave thanks for the food that the earth provided. One of their holidays was celebrated in the fall, after the food was harvested. This was the model for what has become an American national holiday, Thanksgiving. The Woodlanders also built temples, pyramids made out of mud bricks, to serve as burial chambers and also as centers of their religious beliefs. The most famous northeastern tribe is the Iroquois, who have a highly developed society, with villages centering on the longhouse, or community meeting hall and center for religious rituals.

The village life of the Woodlanders was quite different from the roving, warrior bands of the Plains. The Plains Indians are the basis for most of our common stereotypes about American Indians. They are the buffalo-hunting, horseback-riding warriors and hunters. Their vigorous stomp dance is the one that is most often seen at Indian powwows or gatherings (and at Boy Scout jamborees!). The Plains Indians live in teepees, and these homes have become the symbol of Indians across the world. The Plains Indians include the Apaches, Blackfoot, Flathead, and Sioux, to name a few.

The Southwest is home to two different groups of Indians: the Pueblos who live in small villages, farm, and lead a fairly peaceful life; and the Apaches and Navahos, who were warlike hunters. The Pueblos came first, building their towns some 1,500 years ago. The Apaches and Navahos probably came from farther north, driving out some of the Pueblos as they swooped down in a series of raids about 600 to 700 years ago. Later still, the Spanish came, dominating the Pueblo Indians and giving them their Christian religion, but never really subduing the great spirit of the Navahos and Apaches.

Northward, the Great Basin includes the most barren desert lands in the North American continent. Barren land makes farming and hunting nearly impossible; for this reason, the Great Basin Indians became wanderers, constantly searching for seeds, roots, or the occasional wild rabbit to supplement their meager diet. Dry desert lands can't support large communities; the Indians lived in small groups, and everyone had to lend a hand in the search for food.

Blackfoot medecinemen playing eagle-bone whistles.
PHOTO COURTESY:
Smithsonian Institution, Natl. Anthropological Archives

The Northwest Coast Indians offer another startling contrast in life and art. These are the famous makers of totem poles and elaborate masks. Large villages developed, and families grew in wealth and power. The wealthier families owned their own houses and farm implements. Individual families also owned dances and songs that were passed on from generation to generation. The Northwest Indians are famous for their complicated rituals involving the trading of gifts between families; these rituals are called *potlatches*. A family was not only measured by its wealth but also by its generosity in giving freely to others.

Finally, the Arctic Indians lead another totally different life. These are the Eskimos, who probably came very recently to the North American continent from Asia. The Eskimos have developed their own means of surviving in a cold, barren world, creating special tools and methods to fish through frozen lakes.

An Introduction to Indian Music

In our brief survey of the different Indian tribes we have seen that there are many different cultures that are grouped under the name "Indians." You would expect Indian music to reflect these differences, and in fact it does. But, there are also many similarities among the musics of the different Indian groups.

1. Music Is a Part of Religion

Indian music plays a central role in Indian religious ceremonies. The Indians have developed thousands of rituals. Dancing, usually accompanied by vocal music, rattles, and drums, is an important part of every ritual. Not only is music a part of religious ceremonies, the source of music is believed to be the spiritual world. In other words, songs are not composed, but are communicated to gifted individuals by spirits. In some cultures, such as the Navaho, young men must carefully learn to sing each song. The song must be repeated exactly as it is taught, otherwise the spiritual composers will be angered and the good effects of the song will be lost. Other groups, including the Plains tribes, are less fussy about exact repetition of their songs.

Besides religious songs, the Indians also have songs that recount the history of the tribe, songs that accompany social activities such as games, songs to celebrate specific events, like the harvesting of crops, and songs that are known only by members of special secret societies and other limited-membership groups within a tribe.

2. Musicians Are Usually Men

Many societies have sex roles, or specific jobs that are performed by either men or women. Indian tribes are traditionally male-dominated societies; the men usually have all of the power to make laws for each tribe, hunt the food, and conduct the religious ceremonies that include music and dance. Women have their tasks, such as raising food and rearing the young. Songs relating to these jobs will be sung by women, but generally are not considered as important as the religious songs.

3. Indian Songs Feature Nonsense Syllables

When you look at the text of an Indian song translated into English, you'll notice almost immediately that more than half of the words consist of apparently meaningless sounds (called *vocables*). It's as if you were singing a song with the words: "I'm hungry tra-la-tra-la-la, I want some food, uh-huh-uh-huh, right now, yea-yea-yea-yea." It's easy for the Indians to compose new songs; the vocables remain, while new words are substituted for the old.

Indian singers have explained that these apparently meaningless words actually have their roots in a special, spiritual language. Although human singers and listeners cannot understand them, they have great meaning to the spirits, and must be produced precisely in order to please the gods.

4. Indians Alter Their Voices When They Sing

The first thing that strikes you when you hear Indian music is the sound of the singers' voices. Indians often use a shaky voice. The singers usually keep their throats tight, giving their voices an intense, nasal sound (just as you might do by holding your nose and singing at the same time). Indian singers may interrupt their songs with shouts or imitations of animal noises. Indians also often sing in a falsetto voice. In falsetto, the singers reach above their normal vocal range to produce a strange-sounding, high-pitched voice, which is harsher than their ordinary voice.

Of course, different tribes have slightly different singing styles. The Plains Indians use the most vibrato, falsetto, and tight vocal sounds. The Pueblos also use vibrato and a tense, throaty vocal style, but they sing in a lower pitched voice that sounds like the growling of an animal. East of the Mississippi, many tribes sing with little or no vibrato, and keep their vocal chords relaxed, sounding more like the European style of singing that we're accustomed to. The Navaho and Apache sing with much less pulsation than the other tribes. The Great Basin Indians don't use falsetto as much as some of the others.

5. Indian Songs Are Usually Accompanied by Drums

The drum is a central part of Indian religious rituals. It often embodies or contains the voice of the gods, speaking through the drumbeat. The drummer may also direct the movement of the dancers by beating different patterns, which indicate that new parts of the dance should be performed. The Indians have made a wide variety of drums, rasps, and shakers; these will be discussed in the next section.

6. *Indian Melodies and Rhythm*

Most Indian songs are monophonic; in other words, only one melody is sung at a time. Sometimes, when a group of singers sing together, part of the group will sing an octave lower than the other singers. Occasionally, polyphony (or several different melodies sung at the same time) will be heard, but it is rare.

At first, Indian melodies may sound fairly simple. The songs often feature short melodies that are repeated many times, and usually only feature three, five, or six notes. Songs are often split into two parts; in the first half, several short melodies are sung many times. The second half will either feature variations (or slightly different versions) of these melodies, or incomplete repetitions of them. Of course, you may find tribes with more complicated melodies, such as the Woodlanders of the Northeast whose melodies are longer and more complex than those sung by the Plains Indians.

Many Indian melodies begin on a high note and work their way down to lower tones. The Aborigines of Australia have similar melodies. The Indians use call-and-response in their singing; a leader will sing a phrase, and the group will then respond. Sometimes, a leader will sing an entire song, and then the group will sing the same song in response.

The Indians' songs usually follow simple double or triple rhythms (in other words, they have two basic pulses to a measure, or three basic pulses). Although the drumbeat may be steady, the vocalist may keep the melody slightly off the beat, holding back on a note by pausing or extending a note just a little longer than the regular beat would seem to call for. This is particularly true among the Plains Indians, who enjoy hearing this interplay between the singer and drummer. Most songs are accompanied by a percussion instrument, either a drum, clappers (such as bones that are struck together), or rattles.

Iroquois drums
PHOTO COURTESY: Smithsonian
Institution, Natl. Anthropological
Archives

Musical Instruments

The Indians have only a few musical instruments, generally used to keep the beat. These include idiophones (struck sticks or rattles) and membranophones (drums).

The Indians take advantage of the natural world in making gourd rattles. A gourd is almost a natural musical instrument; it has a handle to grasp, and a hollow sphere filled with dried seeds that, when shaken, collide against each other and make a sound. The Indians also make rattles out of leather or rawhide sewn into a pouch or sphere, which is filled with stones or seeds.

The most common membranophone is the single-headed frame drum. A simple wooden hoop is covered with animal hide to make this drum. The frame drum resembles the European tambourine.

One of the most unusual drums is found among the Apache and Navaho. It is the water drum. The water drum usually has a kettle-shaped body that can be made out of any number of materials, such as wood or pottery. The body is filled about halfway up with water, and then a special drumhead is attached to the top. This drum-head is made of tanned leather. When tanned leather gets wet, it tightens and produces a sharp, high-pitched sound. Untanned leather, used on most other drumheads around the world, loosens when wet, and becomes almost impossible to play.

The water inside the drum changes its sound in another way; because there is water inside the resonator (or body of the drum), the size of the resonating chamber is smaller. Imagine an empty glass with a thin piece of plastic stretched across the top. When you strike the plastic, the air inside the glass vibrates. Now imagine that the glass is half filled with water. There is only half as much air in the glass now as there was before. When you strike the membrane on top of the glass, a smaller amount of air vibrates, along with the water.

Although the Indians have many membranophones (drums) and idiophones (clappers/rattles), aerophones (wind instruments) and chordophones (stringed instruments) are less common. Among the aerophones, the Indians have flutes, made either of wood, cane, bark, or, among the Southwestern tribes, pottery. These can have three to six holes and are usually held horizontally. The musician blows into one end of the tube, which can feature a special mouth-piece or notch. The Indians also make single-note whistles from animal bones or wood. Some also play bull-roarers.

The Northwest Indians have probably developed the largest variety of wind instruments. They play an instrument with a double reed placed in the mouthpiece to create the sound; the body of the instrument is made of cedar. According to some musicologists, this is the only native American double-reed instrument. They also have developed many different whistles, flutes, and horns. By taking a fish bladder and attaching it to the mouthpiece of one of these instruments, the Indian can make his own homemade bag-pipes. The air is pumped from the fish bladder into the instrument, rather than being blown from the player's lungs.

The mouthbow is believed to be the only chordaphone that the Indians played before the Europeans came to North America. Indians today play a bowed lute or fiddle, but this instrument was probably made after Indians had seen the European violin.

Music of the Iroquois Longhouse

The Iroquois Indians of the Northeastern United States and Canada have been known since the earliest days of French and English colonization of the New World. They have managed to maintain many of their traditions, through a strong community structure based on the longhouse, a central meeting place named after a long, low-roofed building that serves as church and social center for the individual tribes.

In every season, the tribe must work with the natural world to ensure that the earth will continue to provide abundant food through plants and animals. The religious rituals serve to maintain this link between man and the natural world. For example, in summer, food dances are performed to keep the crops growing, and a special green corn festival is performed to protect the maturing corn from evil spirits.

Other dances have more specific purposes. Shamans or magicians perform certain songs and dances to influence the animal spirits who have the power either to change the weather, or turn the good luck of an opponent into bad luck, or to cleanse a household of disease. Special dances are also addressed to individual food spirits, or animals, or everyday problems.

The best-known Iroquois dance has no specific use, except for enjoyment. This is the stomp dance, and it is known among most Woodlands tribes. The dance is led by a special dancer, who decides which steps will be used, how long the dance will run, how many different phrases (or short melodies) will be sung in the song that accompanies the dance, and how often these phrases will be repeated. Musicologist David McAllester describes the stomp dance:

> The leader conducts the dance as well as the song. As he improvises the calls, he leads a line of dancers in a fast prancing step in time to the music. On the principle of follow-the-leader, when the leader crouches all the others do so too; if he turns in place and then goes on, all the others do so too; if he turns in place and then goes on, all the other dancers do the same. . . . At times the dancers fall into a walk in order to rest. Then the leader starts the fast "stomp" step again and the others follow him.

Iroquois melodies range from single-note songs (or monotones) for special chants to songs with only two notes, all the way up to eight-note songs. The ritual songs tend to have fewer notes, and often will be sung using different "voices", in other words, the singer will purposely alter his voice to make it more intense, or grating, or use a falsetto voice, depending on the specific purpose of the song. In general, the melodies start on the highest note of the song, and then drop down either five or eight notes through the scale. This is a common shape (or melodic contour) for the

Indian with framedrum, c. 1905.
PHOTO COURTESY: Smithsonian Institution, Natl. Anthropological Archives

Plains Indians and other Western tribes, but is somewhat unusual
for an Eastern tribe.

The Iroquois primarily use two different types of musical instruments, rattles and drums. Musical instruments are also associated
with special rituals, and will even be played differently on different occasions. Rattles made from turtle shells are used for special
rituals; they are played differently than rattles made from horn or
bone, which accompany other rituals.

The Plains Indians:
Music of the Blackfoot

The Blackfoot tribes live in western Montana and in the southern
area of Canada directly across the border. The Blackfoot of the
Northern Plains region share many songs and dances with other
Plains tribes. Like other plainsmen, they are horsemen and hunters
and live in small villages of teepees. The tribe is organized around
smaller hunting bands, with one or more leaders, usually tribal
elders. The Blackfoot are particularly skillful hunters and trappers,
and have traded furs with white settlers since the mid 18th century.
Songs help hold the tribes together by giving them a sense of their
special identity. They also serve the same magical functions that
music performs for the Woodlanders.

Plains singers use a higher, stronger voice than their Eastern
neighbors. They also use a pulse or vibrato that gives a gargling or

broken sound to their songs. Melodies usually start on a high note and drop down through the scale, just as in the Iroquois songs.

There are three types of songs: songs based on personal visions, group religious songs, and group social songs. Vision songs usually come to an individual in a dream or trance; they help him pass through difficult stages in his life, and have the power to give the singer renewed strength and good luck. Group religious songs are used to accompany dances for religious ceremonies, particularly ceremonies that honor the sun, and special dances that help cure the sick. Social dance songs accompany the many dances that imitate the natural world (the rabbit and grass dances). There are also songs sung as part of playing games, or even horseback riding.

Not all songs have the same value to the Blackfoot. The ritual songs are most important. They must be performed exactly as they were learned, and traditionally can only be sung to accompany a specific ritual. The melody of each song can only be sung four times at one sitting, although many singers now break this tradition. Second in importance are the songs that belong to the special groups within the tribe. The Blackfoot tribe is divided into seven different groups, based on age. As a person progresses in age and knowledge, he is allowed to learn new songs that go along with his new status.

The songs based on visions or dreams are the next in line in importance. They belong to the individual singer; although others may learn and sing them, they must give credit to the original dreamer as the first person to sing the song. Finally, social songs for dances and games are the least important to the Blackfoot singers.

Like the Iroquois, the Blackfoot primarily play drums and rattles. They use two different types of drum, the common hoop drum with a single head, and a two-headed drum made from a small section of a tree trunk. The trunk is hollowed out and the skin heads are attached at either end. A whistle made out of a hollow eagle's bone is also occasionally seen, along with a few bone flutes.

The Northwest Coast: Music of the Kwakiutl

The Kwakiutl tribes of the Pacific Northwest show an entirely different culture than either the Plains or the Northeastern Indians. Kwakiutl, meaning "beach at the north side of the river," is the group name given to a number of tribes who live in the same general area, along the beaches of British Columbia and Vancouver Island in southwestern Canada. The rivers, bays, and ocean provide

Iroquois rattles.
PHOTO COURTESY: Smithsonian Institution,
Natl. Anthropological Archives

the Kwakiutl with an abundance of fish; wild animals and plants supplement their diet. Without the need for constant scrounging for food, these Indians have developed an elaborate village culture, with lavishly painted houses made of wooden planks, totem poles sometimes reaching sixty feet or more in height, and vast stores of material goods such as canoes, boxes, and other wooden objects. This culture also developed a *hierarchy*, or different ranks within the society; there are chieftains who are the most powerful, commoners who are second in line, and slaves who were owned by the chiefs and had no power.

Musically, the Kwakiutl share with other Northwesterners a unique catalogue of song types. Music is again an important part of religion, but, unlike other tribes where religion is only practiced by the group as a whole, the Kwakiutl family will have its own personal religious practices. Supernatural powers are inherited from father to son, and the songs that accompany these powers often remain within the family. Besides these family-owned songs, there are also religious rituals that cut across the entire tribe, such as the important ceremony of the potlatch, or exchange of gifts, is also accompanied by song and dance. Songs also are sung to celebrate the great deeds of a chief and to recount the legendary acts of past members of a tribe. The Kwakiutl also have healing songs for specific illnesses.

The singing style of the Northwestern tribes tend to be more relaxed than that of the Plains Indians, resembling the vocal style of the East. Songs are limited to three to five notes. The Kwakiutl have developed a unique relationship between the drummers and the singers. The drummer falls slightly behind the vocalist, playing just off of the main beat. This type of accompaniment is called syncopation. The patterns that the various drummers and rattle players create as they accompany the vocalist can become very complex.

The Kwakiutl's most elaborate ceremony is performed at midwinter time. Based on the myth of a young man who must be retrieved from the dead and freed from spiritual forces, the ritual involves elaborate songs and dances. At the time of the midwinter festival, young men are initiated into the tribe, learning special songs and dances that are part of their new level of responsibility as maturing adults. A special leader directs the various songs, coordinating singers, percussionists, and dancers. Although songs vary in structure, they often have two alternating melody parts and are four verses long. In the late 1800's, reports of the wild behavior of the young men during these festivals led the United States government to ban them. Today the songs and dances continue to live even in areas where the festival itself has died out.

The Kwakiutl play a wide variety of rattles, drums, and also beat on planks. Often these instruments are elaborately decorated. Northwestern rattles are often made of wood and are carved and painted to resemble an animal, such as a raven. The availability of hard wood makes it easy to make whistles and flutes that are both loud and long-lasting.

The Indians Today

Indians today live in many different worlds: one is the world of the reservation, separated from the rest of American culture. However, this allows them to enjoy the freedom of some amount of self-government and the opportunity to practice the ancient rituals of music and dance. Other Indians have come into the mainstream, living in American suburbs and cities, working at ordinary jobs, and abandoning ancient beliefs. Still others have left the reservations but continue to attend powwows and other regional meetings to renew their ties with Indian culture.

Indian music has also changed. At almost every powwow, the traditional Indian drums have been replaced by the European bass drum, most often heard in football marching bands. While the older song traditions continue, some Indians have tried to introduce Indian topics and languages into popular styles, such as rock 'n' roll.

The Indians, perhaps more than any other culture we have discussed, have been greatly changed by their contacts with white culture. Many individual tribes were totally exterminated, and their rituals have been lost. Other tribes have abandoned their own rituals to practice the more common rituals performed at the annual powwows; these generally are the dances and songs of the Plains Indians. Recently, interest in Indian culture among both white Americans and Native Americans has led to the revival of some rituals. It is unlikely that interest from outside the tribes will affect the way Indians feel about their culture; the fate of Indian culture rests in the hands of the next generation of Native Americans. It is up to them to decide whether to adapt and change, or to hold fast to their ancient beliefs.

R·E·A·D

General

Curtis, Natalie, *The Indians' Book*. New York: Dover, 1968.

Fichter, George S., *American Indian Music and Musical Instruments*. New York: McKay, 1978.

Hoffman, Charles, *American Indians Sing*. New York: John Day, 1967.

LaFarge, Oliver, *A Pictorial History of the American Indian*. New York: Crown, 1956.

May, Elizabeth (ed.), *Musics of Many Cultures*. Berkeley, CA: University of California, 1980.

Iroquois

Bjorklund, Karna L., *The Indians of Northeastern America*. New York: Dodd, Mead, 1969.

Bleeker, Sonia, *Indians of the Longhouse*. New York: Morrow, 1950.

Fenton, William N., *Songs of the Iroquois Longhouse*. Washington, D.C.: Smithsonian Institution, 1940.

Gridley, M.E., *The Story of the Iroiquois*. New York: Putnam, 1969.

Blackfoot/Plains

Lowrie, Robert H., *Indians of the Plains*. New York: McGraw-Hill, 1954.

Rachlis, Eugene, *Indians of the Plains*. New York: American Heritage, 1960.

Kwakiutl

Drucker, P., *Indians of the Northwest Coast*. New York: McGraw-Hill, 1955.

L·I·S·T·E·N

Handgames of the Kiowa, Kiowa Apache, and Comanche. Indian House 2501.

Healing Songs of the American Indians. Folkways 4251.

Indian Songs of Today. Archive of Folksong, Library of Congress AAFS L36.

Iroquois Social Dance Songs. Irocrafts, no catalogue number.

Music of the American Indians of the Southwest. Folkways 4420.

Music of the Plains Apache. Folkways 4252.

Pueblo Indians. Archive of Folksong, Library of Congress AAFS 43.

Seneca Songs from Coldspring Longhouse. Archive of Folksong, Library of Congress AAFS L17.

Songs and Dances of Great Lakes Indians. Folkways 4003.

Songs and Dances of the Flathead Indians. Folkways 4445.

Songs of Earth, Water, Fire, and Sky. New World 246.

Glossary

General Terms

Aborigine: From the Latin, meaning "from the beginning." The term "Aborigine" is used to refer to a race of people who live on the Australian continent.

acculturation: The process through which a culture loses its own identity and comes under the influence of a mainstream culture, such as Western European culture.

Australoid: The family of brown-skinned peoples found on the Pacific islands.

Caucasoid: The family of light-skinned peoples found in Europe and North America.

clan: An extended family or group of families, usually under the control of a leader or small council of leaders.

culture: All of the customs of a particular group of people, including their music, art, science, habits, and so on.

elima: The female initiation ceremony found among the African Pygmies.

initiation ceremony: A special ceremony or group of ceremonies that marks the change from boy/girlhood to adulthood. Usually occurs at the beginning of adolescence, from age 7 to 12.

karma: The family power and history that is passed on from generation to generation. This term is used to describe certain songs that contain these powers, found among the Australian Aborigines.

mana: The Polynesian/Melanesian concept of a special power that is given to certain objects and people. People with great mana are leaders and enjoy power over others.

moiety: Literally "half." The Australian Aborigines divide their society into two parts, or moieties. Members of one moiety are forbidden to have certain kinds of interactions with members of the other moiety.

molimo: The special male initiation ceremony of the central African Pygmies.

Mongoloid: The family of yellow-skinned peoples, including Asians, Eskimos, and American Indians.

Negroid: The family of black-skinned peoples, originally from Africa, now living in Africa, the Caribbean, the United States, and throughout the world.

potlatch: A ceremonial exchange of gifts practiced by Northwestern American Indians.

primitive: Literally "first people." This word has taken on the meaning of less civilized, barbaric, crude, simple, and bloodthirsty, to name just a few of the negative meanings.

Pygmoid: The class of peoples found in central Africa, the mountains of New Guinea, and other isolated parts of the world. These are usually brown-skinned, short people.

ritual: A special group of customs or ceremonies, practiced by a specific group of people for religious or magical purposes.

tabu: A Polynesian concept originally, tabu has come to mean any forbidden action. Those people or objects that possess mana (see separate reference) are protected by tabus.

tribe: A group of families or clans, bound together by common laws, religion, customs, and the arts. A tribe usually has a recognized leader or group of leaders, often drawn from the oldest members of the various families.

Musical Terms

additive rhythm: A rhythmic structure whereby several different rhythms are joined together, one after the other. For instance, a measure of $\frac{2}{4}$ might be followed by one of $\frac{9}{8}$, then $\frac{8}{16}$, then $\frac{3}{4}$, etc. Compare *divisive rhythm*.

aerophone: The family of musical instruments that create sounds through vibrating air. Examples: flutes, trumpets, reed instruments.

call-and-response: An organization of a song in which a leader or group sings one part (the "call"), followed by a "response" by another singer or a group of singers.

cent: A measurement created by Sir Alexander Ellis to measure the space between tones (called intervals). There are 100 cents between each tone of the equally tempered scale.

chest voice: A form of singing that uses the entire resonating chamber and air power of the chest, lungs, and diaphragm. Compare head voice.

chordophone: The family of musical instruments that create sounds through vibrating strings. Examples: lutes, guitars, zithers, harps.

clef: Written at the left-hand side of the music staff, the clef tells the range of notes that can be written on the staff. Most common are the treble (G) or bass (F) clefs.

divisive rhythm: A rhythmic structure based on a single pulse that is repeated throughout a piece of music. For example, $\frac{2}{4}$ is a duple rhythm. You can divide all of the beats in a measure into two basic pulses. The other common divisive rhythm is a triple rhythm, based on three beats per measure. Compare *additive rhythm*.

drone: A harmony part that consists of one note or tone sung or played at the same time as the melody.

edge instrument: An aerophone with a special mouthpiece that breaks the player's breath into pulses or small, individual bursts of air. Flutes are the most common edge instruments.

electrophone: The family of instruments that creates sounds by electronic means.

equal temperament: The system of dividing the octave into 12 tones, each equally spaced. For example, the space or interval C to C# is the same as the space G to G# (each measures 100 cents; see entry for *cents*).

falsetto: Changing the voice to sing unnaturally higher than normal.

harmony: Literally, different tones played at the same time. In our definition, the harmony part is any other vocal or instrument part that is played to accompany a melody. For different types of harmony, see heterophony, homophony, and polyphony.

harp: The family of chordophones that have an extended neck or yoke, separated from the body. The strings run at a right angle to the neck.

head voice: Vocal sounds produced by using the resonance of the throat, nasal cavities, and skull. The resulting singing voice is sharper and less rich and bassy than the voice produced by drawing on the entire body. Compare chest voice.

heightened speech: A term used to describe songs that are spoken or chanted, rather than sung. The singer alters his normal speaking voice by singing in a different range than his normal speaking voice, or by adding falsetto, heavy breathing, raspy or grating sounds, or in some other manner altering his voice.

hemiola: A rhythmic pattern consisting of 3 measures of 2 beats followed by 2 measures of 3 beats.

heterometric: A changing rhythmic pattern, where the length of the measures in a single piece of music will vary throughout its entire length. Compare *additive rhythm.*

heterophonic: Music consisting of two or more parts that appear to be unrelated to each other.

hocket: A solo or group singing style where the singers either alternate with each other or with a musical instrument, such as a whistle, to produce a melody.

homophonic: A single melody line accompanied by a single harmony part, often consisting of chords.

idiophone: The family of musical instruments that create sounds through the vibration of the entire body of the instrument. Examples include clappers and friction instruments, such as rasps.

interval: The space, or gap, between two tones. For example, the space between C and G is called a fifth, because five scale notes separate C and G (C#—D—E—F—F#). The interval can also be measured in cents (in this case, C to G equals 700 cents).

isometric: A rhythmic pattern in which all measures have the same basic beat and are the same length.

key signature: Used in notation to indicate which notes must be played either sharp or flat to accommodate the basic scale or musical key of the piece.

lute: The family of chordophones that have separate necks from the main resonator/body. The strings of the lute run parallel to the top (or fingerboard) of the neck.

measure: A convenient division of a melody into units based on the meter, or basic rhythm, or a piece. Measures are marked through the use of bar lines.

melody: Musical tones played in succession (one after the other) to create a meaningful composition. Compare *harmony.*

membranophone: The family of musical instruments that create sounds through the vibration of a membrane. Example: drums with skin heads.

monotone: Literally "one note." Monotonal melodies feature only one tone, although variations in vocal quality and the use of slight vibrato and other alterations of the voice can make these melodies sound very rich.

notation: A system of preserving musical compositions in a written form.

overtone: The sounds created by a vibrating string, body, or column of air that are pitched above the primary or loudest sound that is heard. Overtones are created through smaller vibrations that occur as part of the natural property of waves. Sometimes called harmonics or partials.

phrase: A group of notes or tones in a melody that form a logical subunit of the entire melody.

polyrhythm: More than one rhythm being played at the same time.

polyvocality: The ability to alter the singing voice for different songs.

reed instrument: Aerophones that feature small wooden or metal tongues (or reeds) that are set into vibration in order to break up the air column into smaller pulsations.

resonator: An attachment to a musical instrument that is specifically designed to amplify the tone produced by the primary vibrating source. For example, on a violin, the body of the violin amplifies, or makes louder, the sound of the vibrating string.

rhythm: The controlling force behind the duration of the length of time that tones are played in a musical composition. Meter controls the overall flow of beats or pulses in a piece of music.

scale: Any group of tones that are used in a piece of music. This is the broadest definition of scale; in Western music, a scale is a group of 7 notes, usually climbing up in pitch, and usually a whole or half step apart. In non-Western music, scales can have gaps (for example, a scale might be C—E—F#—G—A#), and also often have less than 7 tones (most common are five-note, or pentatonic, scales).

staff: The five parallel lines on which notes are written.

syncopation: A melodic accent that falls off the main rhythmic pulse.

time signature: Used in music notation to show the basic meter of a piece.

trumpet: Any aerophone where the player buzzes his lips against the mouthpiece of the instrument in order to create the vibration in the air column that makes the sound.

vibrato: Manipulation of the voice to create a quavering sound.

zither: The family of chordophones where the strings are stretched across the entire body of the instrument.

Index

DATE DUE			
APR 1 8 '90			
MAY 1 5 '90			
JAN 0 2 '9			